SHAKESPEARE'S SONNETS

The Problems Solved

23
55
130

SOUTHAMPTON AT THE PERIOD
OF THE SONNETS

SHAKESPEARE'S SONNETS

A Modern Edition,
with Prose Versions, Introduction and Notes

by

A. L. ROWSE

THIRD EDITION

MACMILLAN

First published 1964 by
THE MACMILLAN PRESS LTD
Houndmills, Basingstoke, Hampshire RG21 2XS
and London
Companies and representatives
throughout the world

ISBN 0–333–36386–8 hardcover
ISBN 0–333–36387–6 paperback

Printed in Hong Kong

Reprinted 1964
Second edition 1973
Reprinted 1976
Third edition 1984
Reprinted 1991, 1993

To
President Ronald Reagan
for his professional appreciation
of
William Shakespeare

CONTENTS

Introduction to the Third Edition

WHO MR W. H. WAS

All the problems of Shakespeare's Sonnets — for long regarded as the greatest of literary mysteries — have now been solved unanswerably, as in this edition. All of them were solved in my original biography, *William Shakespeare* (1964), except one: the identity of his young mistress, the Dark Lady. I might never have discovered her, if my original findings — the date when the Sonnets were written, the explanation of the publisher's dedication, the identification of Mr W. H., and the rival poet — had not been correct. Discovering the identity of the Dark Lady (when not looking for her) was a bonus for getting all the other answers right, and also for sticking to my last without giving up, in spite of every kind of obtuseness, obfuscation and obstruction.

I must admit that it *is* very difficult for people to get the story of the Sonnets right, the story is so subtle and complex. It is no use people trying their hand — as hundreds have done — or hoping to get it right, unless they are immersed in the Elizabethan age, Shakespeare's own background, and have spent a lifetime of research in it. They simply do not qualify to hold an opinion on these difficulties, beginning with the dating — an indispensable precondition of getting it right. This is where an Elizabethan historian is indispensable, to read the topical references in the Sonnets, which are in logical and intelligible sequence as they are.

Many literary scholars have been all over the place in dating : hence their confusion and the consequent worthlessness of their work. However, it must be allowed that the majority of literary scholars have got the dating right — the Sonnets were written 1592 to 1594/5 — on the obvious, commonsense ground that they were written along with *Venus and Adonis* and *The Rape of Lucrece*, published respectively in 1593 and 1594. The tradition in the main line was right; all my findings are in keeping with it, conservative—and, what is new and original, no less traditional but *definitive*. No need for controversy—mere waste of time—let alone all the confusion from crackpots, some of them making money out of confusing the public's mind. I greatly blame the academic Shakespeareans, who complain at all the confusion they have to contend with, for leaving the gates wide open for the crackpots to canter in, for leaving questions open and uncertain when they have been settled for them—not by themselves but, less surprisingly, by a leading authority on the age in which Shakespeare lived and wrote.

As the very outset there is a stumbling block which has been responsible for a great deal of the confusion: Thomas Thorp, the publisher's, dedication. He had got the manuscript of the Sonnets some fifteen years after Shakespeare had ceased writing them, immersed as he was in the work of the Lord Chamberlain's Company—acting, writing, producing, touring—from 1594 when it was founded. Everybody knows that T. T., Thomas Thorp, wrote the dedication, and scholars know that he was given to writing flowery dedications. He dedicated the Sonnets to Mr W. H., the only person who had got the manuscript—so the crucial point to notice is that *Mr W. H. was the publisher's dedicatee*, not Shakespeare's, who had nothing to do with the publication.

My old friend, Agatha Christie—a good Shakespearean—used to say that everybody misses the significance of the obvious. It is obvious to everybody that Mr W. H. was Thorp's man, and yet almost everybody continues to assume that Mr W. H. was Shakespeare's young man to whom he addressed the Sonnets. How obtuse! when the young lord of the Sonnets is the obvious person, the patron, Southampton. Again, the majority of literary scholars, from Malone onwards, have realised that, without being able to explain the odd dedication.

I must again allow that it is difficult for people to get this right. Even those eminent scholars, Sir Edmund Chambers and Professor Dover Wilson, got it wrong on the assumption that Mr W. H. was Shakespeare's man, not drawing the conclusion from the undeniable fact that he was the publisher's man. Chambers was massively learned but imperceptive; Dover Wilson had bright insights, but was enthusiastic and notoriously erratic. They both of them absurdly plumped for a young lord, on the mistaken assumption that Mr W. H. was Shakespeare's youth.

Everybody knows, or should know, that no lord could be addressed as Mr.   What people do not know, and need an Elizabethan social historian to tell them, is that it was regular social usage to address a *knight* as Mr.   But I have only quite recently learned that it was regular political usage too. Sir Simonds D'Ewes wrote, 'it is usual in this Journal of the House of Commons ... *de an.* 8 and 9 *Regin. Eliz.*, according to the use of former times, to style knights by the term of Mr prefixed only to their surnames.'[1] So Mr W. H. could never refer to a lord, but could refer to a knight. Who was he?

It is obvious that he was someone in close proximity to Southampton, to be the only person who had got the manuscript for Thorp.   Now Southampton's mother, the old Countess, married as her third husband, a young man, Sir William Harvey. When she died in 1607, she left all her household goods and chattels to him.   In 1608 he married a young wife, Cordelia Annesley; this is why in 1609 Thorp is wishing him 'all happiness, and that eternity promised by our ever-living poet', i.e. that which Shakespeare had promised Southampton years before in the Sonnets, if he would marry, have progeny, and carry on the family to posterity.   Thorp called himself 'the well-wishing adventurer in setting forth', in his flowery way, because 1609, the year of publication, was that of the Second Charter to Virginia, by which everybody who was anybody was subscribing to adventure their money, becoming adventurers, in setting forth the first permanent English colony in America.

1607 — 1608 — 1609: this is the answer, the first and unanswerable explanation of Thorp's dedication, which has created so much confusion. It needed an Elizabethan social historian to work it out and solve the problem. Now the way is clear.

---

[1] P. W. Hasler, *The House of Commons, 1558–1603*, I. 13. (*The History of Parliament.*)

SOUTHAMPTON, THE PATRON

That the obvious person, the lordly young patron—he is several times addressed as a lord, virtually described as such in Sonnet 125—was the young man to whom the Sonnets were addressed should have been obvious on logical grounds alone. For, what was the Rival Poet rivalling William Shakespeare for, but the patronage of the patron? That is, the Sonnets were written to and for the patron. Q.E.D. Once more, this is mere commonsense; yet how few people have seen that the Sonnets are patronage poems, written by an Elizabethan poet in course of duty to his patron. They are much more besides—they tell such a strange story, more like a play or a novel when read in sequence, as they should be to understand it and them. Even as such they are utterly exceptional: other Elizabethan sonnet-sequences were not written to a patron, who happened to be a young man, but to the young ladies of their loves, Sidney's Stella, Daniel's Delia, Drayton's Idea, Constable's Diana, etc.: all women.

Here again the majority of literary scholars, from Malone onwards, have known all along that the addressee of the Sonnets was Southampton, but have not known how to explain the confusion created by Thorp with his 'only begetter, Mr W. H.' Others, especially Victorian and Victorian-minded professors, have been embarrassed and fussed by the tone and language of the Sonnets, and wondered whether they were not homosexual.

This was very naif of them, and really quite anachronistic, showing not much knowledge of Renaissance life and manners, the conventions and decorum of Elizabethan society. It was proper for an Elizabethan poet to address his patron or his love in courtly, flowery language—when one addressed the Queen one wrote as if addressing a deity, witness Spenser's *Faery Queene*, or Sir Walter Ralegh's *Book of the Ocean* [Water, i.e. Walter, the l. was not pronounced then] *to Cynthia* [i.e. the goddess, the Queen]. William Shakespeare's language was always rather exaggerated and became extraordinary, elliptical and extreme, later on. (I propose to write about it, in the course of modernising him, making him more intelligible and accessible to moderns, who find the language of 400 years ago too difficult.)

xii

It was appropriate decorum that an impecunious actor-poet should address a star in the Elizabethan firmament, a figure coming to the fore at Court and in society, in polite, deferential, flowery language. Also the youth was beautiful, as beautiful as a woman — and Renaissance people had no Victorian impediment in recognising the fragile and passing beauty of youth, whether in women or men. Witness the contemporary Court poets in France, celebrating the young Henri III as combining both masculine and feminine attributes.

Nevertheless, the Sonnets are not homosexual, as some people would like to think — and others, no less absurdly, fear. Shakespeare makes it perfectly clear in Sonnet 20 that he is not interested in the youth sexually — if only he were a woman! Everything in his life and work shows that Shakespeare was an enthusiastic heterosexual, very susceptible, even inflammable where women were concerned. He was utterly infatuated with the dark young woman, driven 'frantic-mad' by her, as a strongly sexed heterosexual well might be — and his language throughout the Plays shows him the sexiest of writers. The more one knows of Elizabethan language the more of it is revealed to one.

Shakespeare's love for his beautiful young lord was real, and in the Sonnets one can watch its growth and progress; its complications and set-backs; concern, anxiety, regret over the entanglement of the youth with the promiscuous Dark Lady, for which Shakespeare felt himself responsible. It is extremely difficult to get it all right — one needs the pen, or analytical power, of a Benjamin Constant or a Stendhal. One hesitates to use the ambivalent word platonic, or to describe the relationship as 'ideal', when it was certainly real and plunged into uncomfortable depths, distressing for the poet.

There is an unmistakable tutorial tone: Shakespeare was nearly ten years older, the youth without a father, an unsatisfactory man who had treated the charming mother badly, then died leaving the boy heir to the earldom at the age of eight. It was a wonder he was not more spoiled, as Elizabethan aristocrats were apt to be. Head of his family, he would not take on the responsibility of marrying and carrying it on, as everyone urged him to do. He was not as yet responsive to women, when the Sonnets begin as part of the campaign to persuade him to marry; gallant and spirited, he wanted to be free and to shine in action. He had run away at seventeen, from the great Lord Burghley's surveillance as guardian, to serve in Normandy under Essex, his idol, whom he followed in his chivalrous, dangerous course to the gates of death — a suspended death sentence and imprisonment in the Tower. All this came later, contemporary with the heart-ache of *Hamlet* and *Troilus and Cressida*, though the period of patronage — of *Love's Labour's Lost* and *A Midsummer Night's Dream* — had ended, when Shakespeare achieved the independence of becoming a sharer in the Lord Chamberlain's Company in 1594, the generous patron purchasing it for him.

The Sonnets begin in a kind of paradisal innocence, the poet clearly inspired by the society — the world, the power and the glory — opening up for him by the relationship, the opportunity for which his nature yearned and to which it ardently responded. The relationship gets closer, becomes involved, has its strains and disillusionments as is the way in life — it is all very real and recognisable beneath the highly charged, emotional language. No doubt the sensitive poet's heart was touched. He had every reason to be grateful for the fortunate turn his life had taken at last, after the long hard struggle and the discouragements of his earlier life — the Sonnets express again and again his resentment at his lot, that fortune had not done better for him in the lottery. Above all, for a writer, was the inspiration he received from the relationship: 'So are you to my thoughts as food to life', even when regret, reproach, grief come in to play their part, as happens in real life — not in the idealised sequences of Drayton and Daniel.

There are ups and downs in the experiences of these crucial, fateful years, decisive in the life of our greatest writer — and the Sonnets are his inner autobiography. Hence, though a few of the pleasant, non-committal — or not too much committed — ones circulated in the group of friends, they were not for publication, as others' were: too near the bone. After something like a breach comes *redintegratio amoris*, a new theme. At length comes an exhaustion of themes — after more than a century of Sonnets — and an evident cooling-off in the relationship, with the actor fully employed with the new Company and about the country, new associations and demands, frequenting 'unknown minds'.

The patron has some reason to complain; yet Shakespeare insists that there is no 'alteration' in his mind, he constantly recognises Southampton's 'dear-purchased right' in him and his 'great deserts'. Life goes on; the sequence ends appropriately with Shakespeare's assurance that his mind does not change, the affection remains constant. It had never been that of an external honouring the rank and station of a peer, bearing 'the canopy'. His oblation was 'poor but free ... but mutual render, me for thee.' Thus the intimacy ends, with a magnificent but courteous — 'let me be obsequious in thy heart' — assertion of equality, man to man, no breach of tact.

It does not seem that the young Earl and his busy, hard-working poet were together much — perhaps chiefly at intervals over the performance of plays, *Love's Labour's Lost*, which is a private skit on the group, *A Midsummer Night's Dream*, which was shaped up for the Countess's second marriage, to Sir Thomas Heneage on 2 May 1594. Absence was the normal condition for the busy poet, playing, touring, with family demands upon him at home; while a rich young Earl had plenty of other interests and friends to occupy him, in London or in the country. In reading the outpourings of the poet the silence of the patron can be almost heard and felt. It is not to be supposed that the young man was so deeply upset, as was the altogether deeper nature of William Shakespeare, by the triangular imbroglio over the Dark Lady.

There was a reason for this. Though Emilia Lanier got hold of the young peer, he was much more able to defend himself than Shakespeare was — for he was not all that attracted by women: he was bisexual. Even after his forced marriage some years later (1598) — a marriage he tried to get out of — we find him enjoying the embraces of braggadoccio Captain Piers Edmonds in his tent in Ireland.

Here is a complete reversal of situation for people who do not know what they are dealing with; it adds a further difficulty for ordinary minds in understanding the Sonnets and their subtle psychological situation. It was not William Shakespeare, for all his emotional language, who was homosexual; it was the young lord who was ambivalent, not attracted to women until seduced by the experienced Emilia. Shakespeare's very virility may have been an element in the adolescent Earl's attraction to him. We must go no further than that, but it is amusing that the situation is the opposite of that apprehended by the (imperceptive) Victorian professoriate. However, modern minds are better acquainted with this sort of thing, and can understand such a *renversement*.

THE RIVAL POET

Southampton's involvement with Shakespeare's young mistress, stealing 'all my poverty', naturally put a strain upon the relationship. Still the older man felt partly responsible for it; for the rest, beggars can't be choosers, and he ends by forgiving 'the gentle thief':

Take all my loves, my love, yea take them all:

needs must. It was a humiliating situation for the older man between the two young people; but in the conflict between love and friendship — or, in other words, infatuation and necessary duty — friendship won, as in the ending of *The Two Gentlemen of Verona* which critics find so improbable. In these critical years of plague, 1592 and 1593, which closed the theatres, when four or five of his contemporaries and rivals died, Shakespeare was virtually dependent on his youthful, generous patron.

Thus the rivalry with Marlowe for Southampton's patronage was a serious challenge and evidently placed still more of a strain upon the relationship. For, if Marlowe won outright and established a monopoly, Shakespeare tells us that he would be 'cast away', while his life would last no longer than his lord's love and support.

What would happen in this second critical conflict? This part of the story occupies Sonnets 78 and 86 and belongs to the first half of 1593.

We now know that relations between Shakespeare and Marlowe were closer than hitherto realised, and their respective social origins and status contrary to what has been supposed. Here is another difficulty for people unacquainted with the nuances of Elizabethan society. It used to be thought that, because Marlowe was a University man, he was of superior social station. The reverse is true. His father was a Canterbury cobbler, the family distinctly unrespectable; the talented boy went on to Cambridge with Archbishop Parker's scholarship, intended for the Church.

Shakespeare's father, the Alderman, was a leading citizen of Stratford, but the son clearly attached more importance to his mother's family, an heiress in a small way, a sprig of the Arden clan, who were Warwickshire gentlefolk. Alderman Shakespeare spent too much time on the town's affairs, and his own went downhill. The son did not go on to the university: no matter — neither did Ben Jonson, Kyd, Dekker, Drayton, Webster, Chapman or many others whose university was the theatre. William Shakespeare stood out among them all for his determination to be taken as a gentleman, and this was accepted — the epithet regularly applied to him was 'gentle', which meant gentlemanly. But he had hampered himself by having to marry at nineteen, with a wife and three children to support by twenty-one; Marlowe had no such impedimenta, for he was a well-known, indeed aggressive, homosexual.

What importance might that have had in the competition for the adolescent young lord's favour, himself ambivalent, at least homo-erotic? No-one has thought of that, and perhaps few —until today—have understood such complications, certainly not the Victorian professoriate.

Marlowe was only two months older than Shakespeare, but with the early triumph of his *Tamburlane* he was ahead of the actor struggling upwards by writing plays — to the envious Greene's disgust. Marlowe's plays were superior to Shakespeare's early efforts, and so was his poetry. Indeed, so long as he lived, he maintained the lead. In the Sonnets describing the rivalry he is always regarded, not just with courtesy, as superior: that 'abler spirit', that 'worthier pen', he 'of tall building and of goodly pride', while Shakespeare's 'saucy bark' is 'inferior far to his'. Marlowe belongs to the company of the 'learned', whom his junior regards with proper respect and towards whom he evinces an engaging sense of inferiority.

Then, suddenly, the rivalry ends, the rival disappears and is mentioned no more. Sonnet 86 is valedictory, practically all in the past tense: it is all over, luckily for Shakespeare. That Sonnet recognisably describes Marlowe, as my Note on it shows in detail. But those that follow show the strain it had placed on Shakespeare and his relation to the young lord dangerously 'fond on praise'. Things were never quite the same, after these two crises in the story.

Marlowe was killed in the tavern brawl at Deptford on 31 May 1593, after drinking all day with his dubious companions, spilling what genius so wantonly! He left unfinished the poem, *Hero and Leander*, which he was writing in competition with *Venus and Adonis* for the narcissistic young patron's favour. The beautiful youth is recognisably described as Leander in the one, and as Adonis in the other; and there are a number of parallels in phrasing which show that the two poets were aware of each other's work.

Though *Hero and Leander* is unfinished, everyone recognises its superior artistry to *Venus and Adonis*, which we can allow is more comic, more joyously rambling and in that sense gives promise of better to come. Possibly it promises larger potential development, though here we are aided by hindsight: no one can say what Marlowe might have achieved, had he lived.

Here we need go no further in the matter — better to trace the story in the Sonnets and Notes, in the two competitive poems, and the biographies of the poets. For the problem is solved: there need be no further nonsense about Who was the Rival Poet, with such 'candidates' suggested as Gervase Markham, the poet of farriery. Though any suggestion, other than the correct one, is hardly any better.

Once more we must enforce that this finding is in keeping with the tradition: most commentators have realised that Marlowe was Shakespeare's rival for the patronage of the patron. But they were unable to make it certain — what again is obvious — for lack of precise dating. Literary scholars have been all over the place with their dating — quite unnecessarily, for they have realised clearly enough that the Southampton sonnets are closely related to *Venus and Adonis*, which was published in 1593. So why be confused — and confuse other innocents?

The historian has been able to corroborate this commonsense by precise dating from the topical references in the Sonnets and to make it definitive. There never was any justification for wobbling all over the place; now there is no answer, no need for any further discussion. As for being 'controversial' — there is no 'controversy', for there is no rational ground for any other reading of the evidence.

THE DARK LADY: EMILIA LANIER

Shakespeare's affair with this remarkable young lady occupies the last section of the Sonnets in numbering, 127 to 152, though not in time. The affair belongs to 1592–3 contemporaneously with the earlier period of the relationship with Southampton, as Sonnets 34 and 35 show. But the Dark Lady sonnets are different in tone: for one thing they are darker and more upheaved. They are Shakespeare communing with himself about the affair, sometimes light-heartedly, in the end tormentedly, rendered 'frantic-mad' by the young woman, who gives him his dismissal.

All the same the poems were sent to the patron, they were his right — this is what he was paying for, to speak vulgarly. And so they fetched up in the Southampton *cache*, again in an intelligible order. We do not have to exclude the possibility that the young lady herself saw some of the more flattering missives, though that would be mere conjecture. Unlikely, out of the question, that she saw the unflattering, defaming ones; for, as we shall see, when Thorp got hold of them and published them, she was furious and reacted vehemently — in keeping with her temperament as Shakespeare describes her.

The patron was the recipient, as of all that his poet was writing at the time, 'since all alike my songs and praises be, To one, of one, still such and ever so' — no-one else. But the difference of tone is very noticeable, in keeping with the difference between the two objects of his affection, two very different spirits and affairs, one of the mind and heart, the other sexual, torment of body, mind and heart:

Two loves I have, of comfort and despair,
Which like two spirits do suggest me still:
The better angel is a man right fair,
The worser spirit a woman coloured ill.

Whatever stress Shakespeare incurred in his relationship with his
patron, his mind and attitude in the matter are well under control;
in the affair of this strongly sexed man with the young woman he
loses control of himself, he is infatuated, against what he knows to
be her bad character and what other people say about her. For,
notice, he tells us that she is a quite well known person, indeed
notorious; and everything shows that she was a lady of superior
social standing to Shakespeare, if an equivocal one.

The relationship with her is one of infatuation, and everything
shows how sexual it was, even the disgust it aroused by reaction in
himself. Nothing of this in his affection for his young patron. Yet
the New Critic, R. P. Blackmur, got this completely the wrong
way round — thought the poems to the patron were those of
infatuation, when the situation was the exact opposite! If this is all
that critics can do for them, ordinary readers may be excused for
getting mixed up — though they may have more commonsense;
which is also what the Sonnets need for their understanding, along
with a good deal of knowledge of the age and its social nuances,
subtlety of poetic and psychological perception.

It was always commonsense to realise that, since the Dark Lady
was so clearly described as Rosaline in *Love's Labour's Lost* — with
Southampton as the King, Shakespeare as Berowne, Antonio Perez
as Don Armado, and probably Florio as schoolmaster (he was
Southampton's Italian tutor), the young lady was known in the
Southampton circle. We learn subsequently, quite independent-
ly — from the State Papers and Salisbury Mss — that her husband,
Alphonso Lanier, became on friendly terms with Southampton.
She was even better known to the Lord Chamberlain, Lord
Hunsdon, Patron of Shakespeare's Company, for she had been kept
in 'pomp and pride' — so Simon Forman tells us — as mistress of
the great man. Hunsdon was first cousin of the Queen herself,
owning property in Blackfriars, with which Shakespeare was
familiar from these very days; for it was here that his two long

poems were printed in 1593 and 1594 by his fellow townsman from Stratford, Richard Field.

The musicality of the young lady, an element in the spell she put upon the most musical of dramatists, is corroborated by her background. She was the orphan daughter of Baptista Bassano, one of the Queen's Italian musicians, brought up in the ambience of the Court by Susan, Countess of Kent. When pregnant by the Lord Chamberlain she was discarded and married off, with a proper dowry and jewels, to another of the Queen's musicians, Alphonso Lanier. After such grandeur, however equivocal, she looked down on her husband and demeaned him to Forman as a mere 'minstrel'. He was, as a matter of fact, a decent fellow, friend of Archbishop Bancroft (whose hobby, and consolation, was music); but she was given to demeaning other people — she demeaned William. She had reason to be resentful, with her talents and intelligence — that she was highly intelligent, we later find evidence — and with her luck in life. She was now down on her luck, cast down from on high. The susceptible poet fell for her at this moment, out of compassion and pity, a vulnerable state of mind for older men, confronted with distressful youth and beauty:

> If thy unworthiness raised love in me,
> More worthy I to be beloved of thee.

Other emotions entered in, above all sexual passion, though at times Shakespeare — always double- or even treble-minded — was capable of viewing his predicament comically: as in the bawdy 'Will' Sonnets 135 and 136 — now for the first time fully interpreted — which gave such a headache to all the Victorian commentators. These offer an emotional let-up in the increasing tension of the affair, and must have made Southampton laugh, as others of them may have provided a salutary warning, particularly against venereal infection, so common among Elizabethans — it would seem from the end-sonnets that the poet had a touch of it. (So had Robert Greene and George Peele; so had Hunsdon's son, also Patron of the Company as Lord Chamberlain, Forman's acquaintance over many years.)

If we were to look at the affair from the young lady's point of view, she may well have become bored with the sexual fixation of an older man pestering her — sometimes she would consent, sometimes not, as the factual Forman corroborates was his experience later. A rich, unmarried young peer nearer her own age — in 1592 she was twenty-three, Southampton nineteen — was a much better bet.

Shakespeare in the candid way of his 'open and free' nature — no mystery about him — tells us everything about the lady, character and personality, except her name; and the pin-pointing Forman corroborates him in every respect. Promiscuous and notorious; haughty and tyrannical; temperamental and inconstant; a strong personality, mercurial and fascinating, exerting a powerful spell, as Shakespeare specifically says, and Forman adds that she was psychic — as to which we have her own evidence. Years later, when she published her own long poem — for she proved to be a poet too — she tells us that she dreamed up the title, *Salve Deus Rex Judaeorum*, years before she thought of writing it.

Thorp the publisher got hold of the manuscript of the Sonnets after the old Countess of Southampton's death and the legacy of her household goods and chattels to Sir William Harvey, and published them in 1609. The book was not carefully read in proof, as when Shakespeare corrected his own proofs of *Venus and Adonis* and *Lucrece*. The very next year, 1610, Emilia Lanier announced the publication of her long religious poem[1] — she had undergone a conversion in the intervening years, as such ladies are apt to do with the fading of youth and beauty. In 1611 she published it, with a whole series of dedicatory poems to James I's Queen, the Princess Elizabeth, Lady Arabella Stuart, various Countesses whom she did not know, Philip Sidney's sister, Countess of Pembroke; the literary Lucy, Countess of Bedford, the Countess of Suffolk, mistress of Robert Cecil and mother of the horrible girl who, as Countess of Essex, poisoned Sir Thomas Overbury in the Tower. Others she did know: Susan, Countess of Kent, to whom she owed her upbringing; the Countess of Cumberland, so unhappily married to her privateering husband, and their daughter Anne Clifford, to become celebrated as Countess of Dorset, Pembroke and Montgomery. Emilia is as upstage and snobbish as ever, in

[1] *v.* my edition of *The Poems of Shakespeare's Dark Lady*.

spite of being down on her luck.

In between the prefatory dedications and the long poem she inserted a stinging prose riposte to men for defaming women: 'evil disposed men who — forgetting that they were born of women, nourished of women, and that, if it were not by the means of women, they would be quite extinguished out of the world and a final end of them all — do like Vipers deface the wombs wherein they were bred...' Not very Christian of her, her conversion seems incomplete; but clearly she had been rendered furious by the defaming portrait of her in Thorp's publication.

Her poem reveals her as the second best woman poet of the age, after Mary Sidney — much better than the old fashioned doggerel which the Queen wrote. Emilia was a natural poet, who took to rhymed pentameter easily, if somewhat long-winded — as no doubt she had been with Shakespeare and Forman, whom she scared. (The only woman who did, out of many!) She is also a well educated poet, well up in both the Bible and the classics. She has three whole stanzas about Antony and Cleopatra, a subject that appealed to her. Agatha Christie was convinced that, in his unique portrait of Cleopatra, Shakespeare was remembering someone: the essential foreignness, the mercurial inconstancy, the unreliability; the spell she exerted by keeping Antony at heel; the temperament, the tempers; her way of keeping him on edge, or amusing him; the ambition, the courage in adversity. In the stanzas devoted to that couple she is more indebted to Samuel Daniel, whom she knew to whose verse after all hers is more akin; and Daniel had been an acquaintance of both Shakespeare and Florio in the Southampton circle.

What emerges from the poem is still more remarkable, indeed unique: Emilia reveals herself as the outspoken feminist of the age, a foremost candidate for Women's Lib. today. There was indeed no other, certainly no one who so vehemently expressed what she felt. After her experience at men's hands — and not only their hands, but their words — one can sympathise with her, and no less with her resentment at her luck, when she knew herself to be more intelligent and better educated than most of the grand ladies to whom she enviously dedicated her poem.

Throughout the poem she identifies herself with the woman's point of view, with the heroines of the Old Testament, Esther, Deborah, Jael. In her treatment of Adam and Eve she differs from everybody else. All mankind have always held Eve responsible for the curse upon the human race. Not so Emilia: if Adam chose to eat the apple, it was his own fault; it was with the best of intentions that Eve offered it to him, to improve the knowledge he was badly in want of, etc. All this would have been news to John Milton, with his distasteful Puritan view of women's innate inferiority — if he had read the poem, which is unlikely.

For the poem, for all its dedications, was not taken up: it fell flat from the press — or something, or somebody, suppressed it. It is one of the rarest books in the world, only six copies are known to me, three in America, three in Britain, and of these last two are incomplete. When I first discovered the Dark Lady, I did not know of her book: I owe that knowledge to my friends, Lady Mander and Professor Roger Prior, who knows all about the Bassanos and thinks that, like Florio, they were Italian Jews. Some of Emilia's characteristics seem to me to make that likely, at least not improbable.

The Bassanos go on in England today, the Laniers — vastly more numerous — go on in the United States, descendants of the Dark Lady's brother-in-law, Clement.[1] Among them we note the familiar combination of music-poetry-theatre in Sidney Lanier, musician and poet, and Tennessee (Thomas Lanier) Williams, the dramatist.

How corroborative of my findings it turns out to be, that quite unknown to me, the young lady who cast such an unforgettable spell upon our greatest poet should have been herself so remarkable a personality, herself poet and musician, besides then young, beautiful, and unhappy.

But why should her book have fallen still-born from the press, unremarked, for all the attention she tried so hard to win for it — so that it has remained unknown right up to our own day? Still more, why did not Thorp's, *not* Shakespeare's, publication of the Sonnets not receive a proper second edition until a century after-

[1] *v.* Louise Ingersoll, *Lanier. A Genealogy of the Family who Came to Virginia and their French Ancestors in London*. Washington, D.C.

wards? A few had circulated in manuscript, a few had been printed in *The Passionate Pilgrim*. But Thorp's publication of the Sonnets went more or less underground for a hundred years. It is surely very strange, for Shakespeare was the most popular dramatist of the age, his acknowledged poems going into edition after edition.

It has been suggested that the book was suppressed; and the total silence regarding both it and Emilia's book shortly after, taken in combination, makes this all the more likely. After all both Shakespeare and Southampton were now well known public figures, one the foremost dramatist of the time, the other a leading figure at Court, in politics and public life. Neither of them would want the intimacies of their early relations revealed to the public, any more than Emilia relished the portrait of her which the book gave. That it contained the most remarkable sonnets ever written, the intense autobiography of the world's greatest writer, went for nothing: complete silence.

Here is the real mystery: everything else we now know, firmly and unanswerably: no more pointless conjectures. The historian wants to know only the truth, and knows that the truth, about remarkable people — if only one can find it — is far more interesting than the boring conjectures of inferior minds.

SHAKESPEARE'S SONNETS

Never Before Imprinted

—

At London
By G. Eld for T.T. and are
to be sold by John Wright, dwelling
at Christ Church gate
1609

To the only begetter of

these ensuing sonnets

Mr. W. H. all happiness

and that eternity

promised

by

our ever-living poet

wisheth

the well-wishing

adventurer in

setting

forth

T. T.

SHAKESPEARE'S SONNETS

I

From fairest creatures we desire increase
That thereby beauty's rose might never die,
But as the riper should by time decease
His tender heir might bear his memory :
But thou, contracted to thine own bright eyes,
Feed'st thy light's flame with self-substantial fuel,
Making a famine where abundance lies,
Thyself thy foe, to thy sweet self too cruel.
Thou that art now the world's fresh ornament
And only herald to the gaudy spring,
Within thine own bud buriest thy content
And, tender churl, mak'st waste in niggarding.
   Pity the world, or else this glutton be :
   To eat the world's due, by the grave and thee.

I

We desire that the fairest of creatures may increase that beauty may not die out, but as the older in time dies he may leave an heir to carry on his memory. But you, concerned only with your own beauty, feed the flame of life with self-regarding fuel, making a famine where there is plenty : in this you are being too cruel to yourself. You who are just now coming out into the world, a fresh ornament heralding the spring, are burying what you have to give within yourself. Thus are you wasteful in being so skinflint. Take pity on the world, or else be regarded as a glutton — to eat up what is due to the world by dying childless.

———

This sonnet offers the reader no difficulty, except perhaps in the meaning of the last line : 'by the grave and thee' contains two ideas in great conciseness — it refers both to Southampton's dying and to his dying childless. I content myself with drawing attention to the internal rhyme in ll. 1 and 4, and the lovely alliteration in f's that carries through much of the sonnet but is particularly concentrated in ll. 6-8.

2

When forty winters shall besiege thy brow
And dig deep trenches in thy beauty's field,
Thy youth's proud livery, so gazed on now,
Will be a tattered weed of small worth held :
Then, being asked where all thy beauty lies,
Where all the treasure of thy lusty days,
To say within thine own deep-sunken eyes
Were an all-eating shame and thriftless praise.
How much more praise deserved thy beauty's use
If thou couldst answer 'This fair child of mine
Shall sum my count and make my old excuse',
Proving his beauty by succession thine !
    This were to be new-made when thou art old
    And see thy blood warm when thou feel'st it cold.

2

When forty winters have gone by and left deep furrows on you the
pride and flourish of your youth, so much admired now, will be a
rag of little worth. When asked then, 'where is your beauty now?
where is the treasure of your lusty youth?' to answer — 'only
within your own sunken eyes' — were a consuming shame and
profitless praise. To use your beauty would be more deserving of
commendation if you could answer, 'This fair child speaks for me
and makes up my account, a sufficient excuse', his beauty being
yours still in succession. This were to be new-made when agèd,
and see your own blood warm in him when you feel it cold.

———

No difficulty in meaning, except for the conciseness of l. 12. Notice the
double, and paradoxical, use of the word 'livery' in l. 3. It means the
distinctive clothes worn by the servants of some great person ; to apply
it to the young earl's outward appearance is a characteristically Shake-
spearean turn of thought. We learn from the same line that on coming
out into the world, at the age of eighteen, the young earl is much 'gazed
on'.

3

Look in thy glass and tell the face thou viewest
Now is the time that face should form another,
Whose fresh repair if now thou not renewest
Thou dost beguile the world, unbless some mother.
For where is she so fair whose uneared womb
Disdains the tillage of thy husbandry ?
Or who is he so fond will be the tomb
Of his self-love to stop posterity ?
Thou art thy mother's glass and she in thee
Calls back the lovely April of her prime,
So thou through windows of thine age shall see,
Despite of wrinkles, this thy golden time.
   But if thou live remembered not to be,
   Die single and thine image dies with thee.

3

Look in your glass and tell the face you see that now is the time it should form another ; if you do not renew it, you rob the world and some likely mother of a child. For where is the woman whose unploughed womb would disdain your tillage ? Or who is he so foolish as to bury himself in self-love and halt posterity ? You are the mirror of your mother, and in you she calls back the lovely April of her youth. So you, through your own children, may see again this golden time despite the furrows of age. But if you live your life so as not to be remembered and die single, then your image dies with you.

———

No difficulty, except the Elizabethan word 'uneared' in l. 5, which means unploughed. In his dedication of *Venus and Adonis* to Southampton, Shakespeare again used this country word : 'but if the first heir of my invention prove deformed, I shall be sorry it had so noble a godfather, and never after ear so barren a land, for fear it yield me still so bad a harvest'. In 'husbandry', l. 6, there is the double suggestion of cultivating the soil and marriage. In ll. 9–10 Shakespeare takes characteristically courteous occasion for a salute to his patron's mother, the Countess of Southampton.

4

Unthrifty loveliness, why dost thou spend
Upon thyself thy beauty's legacy ?
Nature's bequest gives nothing but doth lend,
And, being frank, she lends to those are free.
Then, beauteous niggard, why dost thou abuse
The bounteous largess given thee to give ?
Profitless usurer, why dost thou use
So great a sum of sums yet canst not live ?
For, having traffic with thyself alone,
Thou of thyself thy sweet self dost deceive.
Then how, when nature calls thee to be gone,
What acceptable audit canst thou leave ?
   Thy unused beauty must be tombed with thee,
   Which, used, lives the executor to be.

4

Thrift of your beauty, why do you spend upon yourself the legacy you have inherited? Nature does not give outright but lends and, being open-handed, she lends to those who are generous. Then why do you abuse the bounteous gifts given you to hand on? Like an unprofitable usurer, why possess such treasures and know not how to live? Trafficking with yourself alone, you deceive yourself. When nature calls you to your rest, how can you render up an acceptable account? Your unused beauty must go into the grave with you, when, if you use it, it will live in your progeny.

The conceit that runs all through this sonnet is that of use and usury, profit and interest, so familiar and pressing a theme to Elizabethans. It is carried ingeniously forward and backward to refer to the looks that Southampton has inherited from his mother, the young man's commerce with himself, the account he will render up at his last audit, his state without leaving himself an executor. There are no difficulties in all this: one can only admire the natural ingeniousness of it. Observe the characteristic Shakespearean reflexive conceit in l. 10, 'Thou of thyself thy sweet self dost deceive'.

5

Those hours that with gentle work did frame
The lovely gaze where every eye doth dwell
Will play the tyrants to the very same
And that unfair which fairly doth excel :
For never-resting time leads summer on
To hideous winter and confounds him there ;
Sap checked with frost and lusty leaves quite gone,
Beauty o'ersnowed and bareness everywhere.
Then, were not summer's distillation left,
A liquid prisoner pent in walls of glass,
Beauty's effect with beauty were bereft,
Nor it, nor no remembrance what it was :
    But flowers distilled, though they with winter meet,
    Lose but their show ; their substance still lives sweet.

5

Those hours that gently shaped the lovely spectacle everyone now gazes upon will prove tyrant and deprive it of its loveliness. For summer leads on to winter, the sap of life is frosted, leaves fall, beauty is snowed over, bareness all round. Then, were no distillation of summer left, like water imprisoned in walls of glass, what beauty can create would be lost, leaving no remembrance even of what it was. But if flowers are distilled, even though they meet with winter, they lose but their bloom; their substance continues sweet.

This sonnet follows up another conceit, which Shakespeare seems to have derived from Sidney's *Arcadia* : 'have you ever seen a pure rose-water kept in a crystal glass ? How fine it looks, how sweet it smells while that beautiful glass imprisons it ? Break the prison, and let the water take his own course, doth it not embrace dust and lose all his former sweetness and fairness ? Truly, so are we — if we have not the stay, rather than the restraint, of crystalline marriage.'

The idea of the distillation of summer is carried forward into *A Midsummer Night's Dream*, I. i. 76-8 :

> But earthlier happy is the rose distilled
> Than that which withering on the virgin thorn
> Grows, lives and dies in single blessedness :

where it is again a reference to Southampton's single state, on the occasion of his mother's marriage to Sir Thomas Heneage, 2 May 1594. In l. 1 'hours' is a disyllable, and should be pronounced, as it is spelt in the original text, 'howers'.

6

Then let not winter's ragged hand deface
In thee thy summer ere thou be distilled :
Make sweet some vial ; treasure thou some place
With beauty's treasure, ere it be self-killed.
That use is not forbidden usury
Which happies those that pay the willing loan ;
That's for thyself to breed another thee,
Or, ten times happier, be it ten for one.
Ten times thyself were happier than thou art
If ten of thine ten times refigured thee :
Then what could death do, if thou shouldst depart,
Leaving thee living in posterity ?
   Be not self-willed, for thou art much too fair
   To be death's conquest and make worms thine heir.

6

Then let not rough winter deface your summer's prime before you leave some essence: distil yourself into some vial, enrich some place with your beauty, ere it be destroyed by you. That usury is not forbidden which makes those happy to pay the loan willingly; that is, for you to breed another like yourself, or — ten times better — ten for one. It were ten times happier if there were ten of you to multiply your image; what could death do then, if you were taken away, leaving you alive in your posterity? Do not be self-willed: you are too fair to be extinguished utterly by death, with only worms for heir.

This sonnet is a kind of antiphon to the one preceding, echoing the images of summer and winter, of summer's distillation and the vial. It also takes up the idea of usury that dominates Sonnet 4, and plays on the statutory limitation on usury at the time to ten per cent. Evidently composed along with these sonnets, it offers a kind of conclusion, and we may regard Sonnets 1-6 as hanging close together in time, forming a first section, a prelude.

7

Lo, in the orient when the gracious light
Lifts up his burning head, each under eye
Doth homage to his new-appearing sight,
Serving with looks his sacred majesty,
And having climbed the steep-up heavenly hill,
Resembling strong youth in his middle age,
Yet mortal looks adore his beauty still,
Attending on his golden pilgrimage ;
But when from highmost pitch with weary car,
Like feeble age, he reeleth from the day,
The eyes, 'fore duteous, now converted are
From his low tract and look another way :
    So thou, thyself out-going in thy noon,
    Unlooked-on diest unless thou get a son.

7

When first the light of the sun appears in the east, earthly eyes do homage to his new appearance, adoring his majesty; and when, like a strong youth in his prime, he climbs up the hill of heaven, mortals still worship his glory, attending on his golden pilgrimage. But when from his zenith he reels down the sky at evening, like feeble age, men's eyes, before dutiful, turn away from his low state. So, if having outstripped your noon you die, you will die unregarded — unless you get a son.

This rather far-fetched and not particularly inspired sonnet — it seems to me to reflect Spenser — reads like a new beginning and starts a new section. The imagery of the sun derives from Shakespeare's classical reading, particularly Ovid. In l. 2 'under eye' means sub-solar, *i.e.* earthly, eye ; in l. 5 'steep-up' means almost vertical, as at midday. The only difficulty is the phrase in l. 13, 'thyself out-going in thy noon', which has the sense of going beyond or outstripping. Most interesting is to note the closeness of l. 14 to *Venus and Adonis*, l. 168 : 'Thou wast begot : to get it is thy duty'. Here is another indication of date : *Venus and Adonis*, published in 1593, would have been written in 1592–3.

8

Music to hear, why hear'st thou music sadly ?
Sweets with sweets war not, joy delights in joy :
Why lov'st thou that which thou receiv'st not gladly,
Or else receiv'st with pleasure thine annoy ?
If the true concord of well-tunèd sounds,
By unions married, do offend thine ear,
They do but sweetly chide thee who confounds
In singleness the parts that thou shouldst bear.
Mark how one string, sweet husband to another,
Strikes each in each by mutual ordering,
Resembling sire and child and happy mother
Who, all in one, one pleasing note do sing :
    Whose speechless song, being many, seeming one,
    Sings this to thee : 'Thou single wilt prove none'.

8

You who are music to hear, why are you sad to hear it ? Joy does not conflict with joy : why do you love that which you receive not gladly or else receive with pleasure what disturbs you? If the harmony of well-tuned sounds married together offends your ear, they reproach you for keeping in unison the several parts that you should bear.   Mark how one string, wedded to another, strikes each one in mutual order — just like father, mother, child, who sing together all in one pleasing note.   Their wordless voices, together sounding one, sing this to you : 'Single, you will come to nothing'.

––––––

This sonnet changes the metaphor to music and tackles the young man from another side.   We know that Shakespeare loved music, but Southampton's attitude is described here as ambivalent.   If he liked it, nevertheless it disturbed him.   Well it might, for its harmony of sounds married together was a reproach to his single state : such is the theme, ingeniously worked out.   The only difficulty is in the conciseness of the phrase in the last line, 'thou single wilt prove none', which relates to the popular phrase, 'one and none is all one'.   Observe in l. 8 the characteristic suggestiveness of the word 'bear', *i.e.* to bear or carry a part, to bear the burden, in music or in life, to bear children.   Years later, something of l. 14, long dormant in Shakespeare's mind, came to the surface again in *The Phoenix and the Turtle*, l. 28 : 'Number there in love was slain'.

9

Is it for fear to wet a widow's eye
That thou consum'st thyself in single life ?
Ah, if thou issueless shalt hap to die
The world will wail thee like a mateless wife ;
The world will be thy widow and still weep
That thou no form of thee hast left behind,
When every private widow well may keep,
By children's eyes, her husband's shape in mind.
Look, what an unthrift in the world doth spend
Shifts but his place, for still the world enjoys it ;
But beauty's waste hath in the world an end
And, kept unused, the user so destroys it.
   No love toward others in that bosom sits
     That on himself such murd'rous shame commits.

9

Is it for fear of leaving a widow to grieve that you consume your life in the single state ? But, if you happen to die issueless, the world will be your widow and grieve that you have left no pattern of yourself behind — when every private widow may keep her husband's shape in mind through their children. Look, what a waster in the world throws away is but handing it over to someone else, for still the world enjoys it; but the waste of beauty makes a final end for, if it is not put to use, it is destroyed by its possessor. There is no love towards others in the bosom of one who commits such a crime upon himself.

———

This pushes forward the theme now from another side, putting another aspect of the case. In l. 4 the original phrase is 'makeless wife' : cf. the medieval carol, 'I sing of a maiden that is makeless'. The modern equivalent of this is 'mateless'. Observe the alliteration in w's that runs through practically the whole sonnet and fortifies it. Ll. 11-12 have an obvious parallel in Marlowe's *Hero and Leander*, I. 328 : 'Beauty alone is lost, too warily kept'. And this, considering what we now know about the nature of this poem and its relation to Southampton, is significant. Cf. my *Shakespeare the Man*, 76 foll.

10

For shame deny that thou bear'st love to any
Who for thyself art so unprovident.
Grant, if thou wilt, thou art beloved of many,
But that thou none lov'st is most evident :
For thou art so possessed with murd'rous hate
That 'gainst thyself thou stick'st not to conspire,
Seeking that beauteous roof to ruinate
Which to repair should be thy chief desire.
O, change thy thought, that I may change my mind !
Shall hate be fairer lodged than gentle love ?
Be, as thy presence is, gracious and kind,
Or to thyself at least kind-hearted prove :
 Make thee another self, for love of me,
 That beauty still may live in thine or thee.

10

Deny it for shame that you love any, when you are so improvident
of yourself. Grant that there are many who love you, still it is clear
that you love none: for you are possessed with hate, to conspire
against yourself like this, seeking to ruin that splendid house which
it should be your chief desire to repair. Reverse your course, that I
may change my mind! Should hate be lodged in a fairer shell than
love? Be true to yourself, be gracious and kind, as your appearance
is, or at least be kind-hearted to yourself. Make you another self,
for love of me, that your beauty may live on in you and yours.

In this sonnet Shakespeare speaks out for the first time in his own person ;
for the first time he says 'I', and 'Make thee another self, for love of me'.
Evidently his emotion has been touched, and this can be felt in the more
intimate and personal language of the poem. We must not exclude the
possibility that the poet had been called in by the young Earl's mother to
aid her in her campaign of persuading her son to marry and carry on his
house. This is the point of ll. 7-8 : it was Southampton's duty to repair
the fortunes of his family, damaged by his father's extravagance, jeopar-
dised by its Catholicism, and make its future safe.

One notes the tone of polite exaggeration, almost in inverted commas,
by now a kind of banter, almost a game between them. For now Shake-
speare's own feelings are becoming engaged : *he* has been caught by the
young lord's charm.

From the point of view of dating it is important to note that l. 7 has
close parallels in Shakespeare's first two comedies : cf. *The Comedy of
Errors*, III. ii. 4, 'Shall love, in building, grow so ruinous' ; and *The Two
Gentlemen of Verona*, V. iv. 9, 'Lest, growing ruinous, the building fall'.

23

II

As fast as thou shalt wane so fast thou grow'st
In one of thine from that which thou departest,
And that fresh blood which youngly thou bestow'st
Thou may'st call thine when thou from youth convertest.
Herein lives wisdom, beauty, and increase,
Without this, folly, age, and cold decay :
If all were minded so the times should cease
And threescore year would make the world away.
Let those whom nature hath not made for store,
Harsh, featureless and rude, barrenly perish :
Look, whom she best endowed she gave the more,
Which bounteous gift thou shouldst in bounty cherish :
   She carved thee for her seal, and meant thereby
   Thou shouldst print more, not let that copy die.

II

As fast as you wane so will you grow in a child of yours, from that which you planted : the fresh blood you gave you may still call yours when youth departs. This is wisdom, beauty, and increase : without it, folly, age, decay. If all were minded like you the world would come to an end in man's threescore years. Let those whom nature has not made to breed from — harsh-featured and rough — perish without offspring. Look, to whom she gave so much she gave even more : the bounteous gift she gave you should in bounty cherish. She made you for her seal, intending that you should print more from it, not let the pattern die.

———————

Little comment is necessary, except that the word 'departest' in l. 2 offers some difficulty. With the Elizabethans it had the secondary sense of parting with, or giving away : hence my rendering. We have the authority of the Psalmist for holding that 'the days of our age are threescore years and ten'. The Psalms are constantly reflected throughout Shakespeare, most often in the Prayer Book version, which he would have heard in church all his life.

12

When I do count the clock that tells the time
And see the brave day sunk in hideous night,
When I behold the violet past prime
And sable curls all silvered o'er with white,
When lofty trees I see barren of leaves,
Which erst from heat did canopy the herd,
And summer's green all girded up in sheaves
Borne on the bier with white and bristly beard :
Then of thy beauty do I question make
That thou among the wastes of time must go,
Since sweets and beauties do themselves forsake
And die as fast as they see others grow :
    And nothing 'gainst Time's scythe can make defence
    Save breed, to brave him when he takes thee hence.

12

When I count the clock and see bright day sunk into night, when I behold the violet withering or dark curls streaked with silver; when I see the trees stripped of their leaves, which earlier canopied the herd from heat, and summer's green corn girded up in sheaves and borne on the bier white and bearded — then, thinking of you, I wonder whether you must go along with time's waste, since all lovely things die as fast as they see others grow. There is no defence against time's scythe save to breed, to confront him when he takes you away.

———

Here is Shakespeare the countryman born and bred. The pastoral picture of ll. 5-8 suggests that this was written in the country after the barley-harvest. Notice for dating that the collocation of shade and canopy appears in *3 Henry VI*, II. v. 42-5 :

> Gives not the hawthorn bush a sweeter shade
> To shepherds, looking on their silly sheep,
> Than doth a rich embroidered canopy
> To kings ?

While ll. 7–8 have a close parallel in *A Midsummer Night's Dream*, II. i. 94–5;

> the green corn
> Hath rotted ere his youth attained a beard.

O, that you were yourself ! but, love, you are
No longer yours than you yourself here live :
Against this coming end you should prepare
And your sweet semblance to some other give.
So should that beauty which you hold in lease
Find no determination : then you were
Yourself again, after yourself's decease,
When your sweet issue your sweet form should bear.
Who lets so fair a house fall to decay,
Which husbandry in honour might uphold
Against the stormy gusts of winter's day
And barren rage of death's eternal cold ?
    O, none but unthrifts : dear my love, you know
    You had a father : let your son say so.

O, that you were yourself! but, love, you are no longer yours than you remain alive : against this inevitable end you should prepare by handing on your semblance to another. Thus should that beauty of which you have but a lease not come to an end : thus, after your death, you would live again in the form of your offspring. Who lets so fine a house fall into ruin, when honour itself in marriage might uphold it against the storms of winter, the bleak eternal cold of death? None but wasters. My love, you yourself had a father : let your son say as much.

———

This sonnet marks a second stage in the growth of Shakespeare's feelings : the youth is addressed as 'love' and 'dear my love'. In l. 10, once more 'husbandry' is used in both senses and again Southampton's duty not to let his house fall into decay is enforced — the more compellingly for the reference, in the last couplet, to Southampton's dead father : all now rests on the son to continue the house.

Observe again the close parallel with *Venus and Adonis*, ll. 171 foll. :

Upon the earth's increase why shouldst thou feed,
Unless the earth with thy increase be fed ?
By law of nature thou art bound to breed,
That thine may live when thou thyself art dead ;
And so, in spite of death, thou dost survive,
In that thy likeness still is left alive.

14

Not from the stars do I my judgment pluck,
And yet methinks I have astronomy,
But not to tell of good or evil luck,
Of plagues, of dearths, or seasons' quality ;
Nor can I fortune to brief minutes tell,
Pointing to each his thunder, rain and wind,
Or say with princes if it shall go well,
By oft predict that I in heaven find.
But from thine eyes my knowledge I derive,
And, constant stars, in them I read such art
As — truth and beauty shall together thrive
If from thyself to store thou wouldst convert ;
   Or else of thee this I prognosticate :
   Thy end is truth's and beauty's doom and date.

14

I do not judge by the stars, though I have astronomy enough, but not to tell fortunes, or foretell plagues, dearths, or the seasons' weather. Nor can I say from minute to minute what the time will hold, thunder, rain or wind; or prophesy how it will go with princes, predict by frequent portents what I find in the heavens. I derive my knowledge from your eyes: they are my constant stars, in which I read such a lesson as that truth and beauty will thrive together if only you would turn from yourself to breeding. Otherwise my prophecy is that your end is a doom upon truth and beauty.

———

After all the comparisons, metaphors, images, turns of thought we have had — the seasons, summer and winter, the green corn and the corn white unto the harvest, the concord of music, the looking-glass, the vial, the seal and its imprint — Shakespeare thinks of yet another variation for his theme, on astronomy. The suggestion is thought to come from his reading of Sidney. The age was much given to astrology, and the 1590s in particular to prognostications and almanacs with their forecasts. This sonnet has the first reference to the plague that raged in these years 1592 and 1593. L. 9 is closely paralleled in *Love's Labour's Lost*, of 1593–4, IV. iii. 350 : 'From women's eyes this doctrine I derive'.

15

When I consider every thing that grows
Holds in perfection but a little moment,
That this huge stage presenteth nought but shows
Whereon the stars in secret influence comment ;
When I perceive that men as plants increase,
Cheered and checked even by the self-same sky,
Vaunt in their youthful sap, at height decrease,
And wear their brave state out of memory :
Then the conceit of this inconstant stay
Sets you most rich in youth before my sight,
Where wasteful Time debateth with Decay,
To change your day of youth to sullied night :
   And all in war with Time for love of you,
   As he takes from you, I engraft you new.

15

When I consider that every thing that grows has but a brief
moment of perfection, that the world is but a stage upon whose
shows the stars exert their influence secretly; when I observe that
men increase like plants, nourished or checked by these same skies,
flaunt themselves in the sap of youth, then at their full height begin
to decline, so that their brave prime vanishes out of mind: then the
thought of this unceasing change brings your youth richly before
my eyes, where wasteful time debates with decay to change the
daytime of your youth to dark night: engaged in my war with
Time for love of you, as he takes from you I build you up anew.

———

This sonnet marks a further stage in the progress of Shakespeare's affec-
tion : the last couplet is the first adumbration of the theme of the immor-
tality the poet will confer on the young man — as he did — by his verse.
L. 3 gives us Shakespeare's first reference to the world as a stage, with its
reflection of his profession, of which we shall hear a great deal more as
the sonnets go on. L. 12 has a parallel in *Richard III*, IV. iv. 16 : 'Hath
dimmed your infant morn to agèd night'.

16

But wherefore do not you a mightier way
Make war upon this bloody tyrant, Time ?
And fortify yourself in your decay
With means more blessèd than my barren rhyme ?
Now stand you on the top of happy hours,
And many maiden gardens, yet unset,
With virtuous wish would bear your living flowers,
Much liker than your painted counterfeit :
So should the lines of life that life repair,
Which this time's pencil, or my pupil pen,
Neither in inward worth nor outward fair,
Can make you live yourself in eyes of men.
   To give away yourself keeps yourself still ;
   And you must live, drawn by your own sweet skill.

16

But why do you not take a more effective way of defeating tyrant time? And fortify yourself against decay by better means than my barren verse? Now you stand at the top of happy hours, and many virginal gardens, as yet not planted, would willingly bear your living flowers, much more like you than your painted portrait. So should the living lineaments of you bring you to mind as neither your portrait nor my pen, describing outward appearance or inner worth, can make you live in men's eyes. To give yourself away is a means of preserving yourself: you can then live on, drawn by your own skill.

———

Southampton was painted about this time : we have a Hilliard miniature of him from the period of the Sonnets. This perhaps suggested the comparison, the figure, that runs through this poem; the phrase in l. 10, 'this time's pencil' may be a specific reference to Hilliard. Ll. 10-11 offer some difficulty through the conciseness of their expression, and there are disputed interpretations of their punctuation and meaning. I give what I take to be the sense of them. L. 14 reflects a line from Sidney's *Arcadia* : 'With his sweet skill my skilless youth he drew'.

17

Who will believe my verse in time to come
If it were filled with your most high deserts ?
Though yet heaven knows it is but as a tomb
Which hides your life and shows not half your parts.
If I could write the beauty of your eyes
And in fresh numbers number all your graces,
The age to come would say, 'This poet lies :
Such heavenly touches ne'er touched earthly faces'.
So should my papers, yellowed with their age,
Be scorned like old men of less truth than tongue,
And your true rights be termed a poet's rage
And stretchèd metre of an antique song :
    But were some child of yours alive that time,
    You should live twice, in it and in my rhyme.

17

Who will believe my verse in time to come if it were filled with
your great deserts?—though it but conceals your life and portrays
not half your gifts. If I could describe the beauty of your eyes and
in fresh numbers number all your graces, the next age would not
believe me and would say that such heavenly touches never graced
earthly countenances. And my writings, yellow then with age,
would be scorned like babbling old men, and untruthful: your due
praise would be termed a poet's fantasy, the forced strains of an old
song. But were some child of yours alive then, you should have a
double life, in it and in my verse.

———

This rather conventional sonnet offers no difficulties. Perhaps I may
point out that 'deserts' in l. 2 rhymes with 'parts' in l. 4, since in earlier
days 'er' was regularly pronounced 'ar', as in serjeant or clerk (in Eng-
land) today.

18

Shall I compare thee to a summer's day ?
Thou art more lovely and more temperate :
Rough winds do shake the darling buds of May,
And summer's lease hath all too short a date :
Sometime too hot the eye of heaven shines,
And often is his gold complexion dimmed ;
And every fair from fair sometime declines,
By chance or nature's changing course untrimmed.
But thy eternal summer shall not fade,
Nor lose possession of that fair thou ow'st ;
Nor shall death brag thou wander'st in his shade,
When in eternal lines to time thou grow'st :
　　So long as men can breathe, or eyes can see,
　　So long lives this, and this gives life to thee.

18

Shall I compare you to a summer's day? You are more gracious and more gentle. Rough winds shake the buds of May, and the lease of summer is all too short: sometimes the sun is too hot, or often is clouded over; everything that is fair loses its beauty, by chance or in the course of nature coarsened. But your eternal summer shall not fade, nor lose the beauty that belongs to it; nor shall death boast possession of you, when in eternal verse you grow one with time. So long as men can breathe, or eyes can see, so long will this live, giving you immortality.

———

This first of the Sonnets to become very famous sets a difficult problem in turning it into prose ; for the most part one can only repeat its language, perfectly direct and straightforward : no problems of interpretation. One can but notice the inspired nature of the poem : it is the certainty of love, that brings with it Shakespeare's confidence in the immortality of his verse. Though a convention with Renaissance poets, it was in this case prophetically justified.

19

Devouring Time, blunt thou the lion's paws,
And make the earth devour her own sweet brood ;
Pluck the keen teeth from the fierce tiger's jaws,
And burn the long-lived phoenix in her blood ;
Make glad and sorry seasons as thou fleet'st,
And do whate'er thou wilt, swift-footed Time,
To the wide world and all her fading sweets :
But I forbid thee one most heinous crime —
O, carve not with thy hours my love's fair brow,
Nor draw no lines there with thine antique pen ;
Him in thy course untainted do allow
For beauty's pattern to succeeding men.
   Yet do thy worst, old Time : despite thy wrong,
   My love shall in my verse ever live young.

19

Time that devours all, blunt the lion's paws, and make the earth
consume her creatures; take away the tiger's sharp tooth, and let
the phoenix burn alive in her ashes. Swift Time, make happy or
sad seasons as you fly, and do what you will to the world and all its
fading charms. But I forbid you one crime — mark not my love's
brow with your traces, nor draw your lines upon it: allow him to
go unscathed, for a pattern of beauty to succeeding generations.
Yet, do your worst: despite Time's injury, my love shall live ever
young in my verse.

————

This somewhat laboured poem, developing an Elizabethan commonplace,
is an antiphon to the preceding, thought up as a kind of consequence to
that inspired sonnet. Not all a poet's verse can be expected to be inspired.
However, the animal imagery has its quaint curiosity, and reminds one
of the animal-woodcuts of the time, Topsell's for instance. And Shake-
speare's concern with Time, as a destroyer of youth and beauty, is a
fundamental theme of the Southampton sonnets. Hyder Rollins observes,
New Variorum Edition of Shakespeare. The Sonnets, ll. 52-3 : 'it seems
worth noting that the word *time* is used seventy-eight times in 1-126 and
not once in the remaining sonnets. Rearrangers have not always observed
this fact.'

20

A woman's face with Nature's own hand painted
Hast thou, the master-mistress of my passion ;
A woman's gentle heart, but not acquainted
With shifting change, as is false women's fashion ;
An eye more bright than theirs, less false in rolling,
Gilding the object whereupon it gazeth ;
A man in hue, all hues in his controlling,
Which steals men's eyes and women's souls amazeth.
And for a woman wert thou first created,
Till Nature, as she wrought thee, fell a-doting,
And by addition me of thee defeated,
By adding one thing to my purpose nothing ;
   But since she pricked thee out for women's pleasure,
   Mine be thy love, and thy love's use their treasure.

20

You have a woman's face, with Nature's own colouring, you who
are the master-mistress of my love ; a woman's gentle heart, but
not changeable as is the way with women ; an eye brighter than
theirs, more sincere, lighting up the object it looks upon. A man in
complexion, all complexions at his command, which attracts men's
eyes as it steals women's hearts. And for a woman were you first
intended, till Nature slipped up in making you and, by adding one
thing of no use to me, defrauded me of you. But since she
equipped you for women's pleasure, let them have it, so long as I
may have your love.

———

This crucial sonnet gives the key to the nature of Shakespeare's love for
the young man, and shows that it was not homosexual. He does not
want to possess him physically : he is defeated by Southampton's being
of the male sex. If only he were a woman, as he is like one in his youthful
appearance, Shakespeare repines ! Southampton is portrayed as a feminine
youth with something of the qualities of both sexes ; and this in fact was
the case : ambivalent in his youth, there is some evidence of his response
to both sexes, even after his somewhat belated marriage.

It is not worth commenting on the vast amount of nonsense this sonnet
has given rise to, when it is perfectly clear what it says and what it means.
The pun in 'pricked' in l. 13 is meant to be enjoyed.

21

So is it not with me as with that Muse,
Stirred by a painted beauty to his verse,
Who heaven itself for ornament doth use
And every fair with his fair doth rehearse,
Making a couplement of proud compare,
With sun and moon, with earth and sea's rich gems,
With April's first-born flowers, and all things rare
That heaven's air in this huge rondure hems.
O, let me, true in love, but truly write,
And then believe me, my love is as fair
As any mother's child, though not so bright
As those gold candles fixed in heaven's air :
    Let them say more that like of hearsay well ;
    I will not praise that purpose not to sell.

21

I am not like that poet, inspired to write by a painted beauty, who calls upon heaven itself for decoration, adduces everything lovely for comparison, sun and moon, earth and sea, April flowers, everything rare that the heavens circle in this world. True in love, let me but write the truth: my love is as fair as any mother's child, though not so bright as the golden candles in the sky. Let them say more that prefer rumour: I will not cry up what I do not propose to sell.

It is clear that this Sonnet refers to Sir Philip Sidney — a chief influence on Shakespeare's early work — and his famous sonnet sequence, *Astrophil and Stella*, which started the sonneteering vogue of the 1590s. Sidney's praise of Stella calls upon sun, moon, stars (of course), and spring flowers. Stella was Lady Penelope Rich, Essex's sister, famous for her brilliant complexion, no doubt improved by art. L.8: observe the internal rhyme 'air' with 'rare': Shakespeare had that obvious first sign of the born poet, spontaneous facility in rhyming. L. 14 is reflected in *Love's Labour's Lost*, IV. iii. 240, 'To things of sale a seller's praise belongs'.

22

My glass shall not persuade me I am old,
So long as youth and thou are of one date ;
But when in thee time's furrows I behold
Then look I death my days should expiate.
For all that beauty that doth cover thee
Is but the seemly raiment of my heart,
Which in thy breast doth live, as thine in me :
How can I then be older than thou art ?
O therefore, love, be of thyself so wary
As I, not for myself, but for thee will,
Bearing thy heart, which I will keep so chary
As tender nurse her babe from faring ill.
   Presume not on thy heart when mine is slain :
   Thou gav'st me thine not to give back again.

22

When I look in the glass I shall not be persuaded that I am old, so long as you are young; but when I see time's furrows in you, then I expect death to expiate my days. For all your external beauty is but the garment of my heart, which lives in your breast, as yours in mine: how can I then be older than you? Then, love, be as careful of yourself as I will be of you — not for myself, but since I have your heart, which I will keep as tenderly as a nurse keeps her babe from harm. Do not expect your heart back when I am dead: you gave me yours not to give back again.

———

The new image of this sonnet is that of an exchange of hearts between Shakespeare and his young friend: the assumption is therefore that the latter returns Shakespeare's affection. We observe, after the conventional character of the preceding sonnet, the intimate language of this, which betokens a further progress in their relations. The psychological interest of the poem is obvious — with the older man trying to persuade himself against the difference of age between them. In this year 1592 Shakespeare was twenty-eight, for an Elizabethan no longer young; Southampton was not yet nineteen. Yet we observe a certain tutorial sentiment in ll. 11-12, as if Shakespeare felt himself *in loco parentis*. L. 7 has a close parallel in *Love's Labour's Lost*, V. ii. 825, 'my heart is in thy breast'.

23

As an unperfect actor on the stage
Who with his fear is put beside his part,
Or some fierce thing replete with too much rage,
Whose strength's abundance weakens his own heart :
So I, for fear of trust, forget to say
The perfect ceremony of love's rite,
And in mine own love's strength seem to decay,
O'ercharged with burden of mine own love's might.
O, let my books be then the eloquence
And dumb presagers of my speaking breast,
Who plead for love and look for recompense
More than that tongue that more hath more expressed.
    O, learn to read what silent love hath writ :
    To hear with eyes belongs to love's fine wit.

truth,
judgement,
wisdom

Like an imperfect actor on the stage who is put out of his part with fright, or is too much moved with passion and so weakens his effect: so I, fearing to trust myself, forget to give the full and proper expression of devotion due to love, and filled with too much feeling appear to falter. Let my works then speak up for me, the dumb witnesses of my heart: who plead for love and look for recompense greater than that tongue that has more fully expressed greater ardours. Learn to read then what silent love has written: to hear with one's eyes is a fine point of wit in love.

can't express him self conventionally so does it through his sonnet!

This sonnet gives us Shakespeare's first extended reference to his own profession as actor, and very effective use he makes of it for a comparison to express his own natural diffidence in the relationship with the young peer. We may infer from it, too, that few words had passed between them on the subject, and that Shakespeare's chief appeal to Southampton was with and through his poems, his 'books', and that so far it was rather a 'silent love'. Only l. 12 presents any difficulty; it refers again to Sidney's volubly expressed ardour for Stella, which in fact received no 'recompense'. Shakespeare hopes for more from Southampton.

Actor vs. Lover
too much emotion

24

Mine eye hath played the painter and hath stelled
Thy beauty's form in table of my heart ;
My body is the frame wherein 'tis held,
And perspective it is best painter's art.
For through the painter must you see his skill
To find where your true image pictured lies,
Which in my bosom's shop is hanging still
That hath his windows glazèd with thine eyes.
Now see what good turns eyes for eyes have done :
Mine eyes have drawn thy shape, and thine for me
Are windows to my breast, where-through the sun
Delights to peep, to gaze therein on thee :
    Yet eyes this cunning want to grace their art,
    They draw but what they see, know not the heart.

24

My eye had played the painter and limned your form upon the palette of my heart; my body is the frame of the picture: it is the best painter's art to give it perspective. Through the painter's skill you must look to find where your true image lies depicted: it hangs in my breast like a picture in a shop, whose windows are glazed with your eyes. See what good turns eyes have done for each other: mine have drawn your image, and yours are windows into my breast, through which the sun delights to peep, gazing on you there. Yet eyes lack this knowledge: they draw only what they see, they do not know the heart.

A rather far-fetched conceit in the Elizabethan manner, yet the sincerity shines through the artifice. It reveals Shakespeare becoming more cultivated, with life in London and introduction into the circle of Southampton House — interested in painted portraits, a feature of the age.

25

Let those who are in favour with their stars
Of public honour and proud titles boast,
Whilst I, whom fortune of such triumph bars,
Unlooked for joy in that I honour most.
Great princes' favourites their fair leaves spread
But as the marigold at the sun's eye,
And in themselves their pride lies burièd,
For at a frown they in their glory die.
The painful warrior famousèd for fight,
After a thousand victories once foiled,
Is from the book of honour razèd quite,
And all the rest forgot for which he toiled :
    Then happy I, that love and am beloved
    Where I may not remove nor be removed.

25

Let those who are favoured by luck boast of public honours and titles, while I, deprived of such things by fortune, take unlooked-for joy in what I honour most. The favourites of princes spread their glory, like the marigold only when the sun shines on them; their pride dies in them, for at a frown they are cast away. The famous warrior, after all his battles once caught out, is razed from the book of honour and all his services forgotten. How fortunate them am I to love and be beloved where I may neither change nor be rejected.

This extremely revealing sonnet has a double importance for us. First, it reveals Shakespeare's feelings about the restricted circumstances of his birth and fortune. Second, it refers to Sir Walter Ralegh's fall from favour and disgrace, which was the sensation of the summer of 1592. The very phrases closely describe Ralegh's situation and personality : the emphasis on his services and his toil — he can 'toil terribly', Sir Robert Cecil wrote of him at just this juncture. Ralegh himself wrote, 'once amiss hath bereaved me of all' — a phrase reflected in 'once foiled', cf. my *Ralegh and the Throckmortons*, p. 163. In l. 9 'painful' means painstaking, hard-working : a well-recognised characteristic of Ralegh's.

26

Lord of my love, to whom in vassalage
Thy merit hath my duty strongly knit,
To thee I send this written ambassage
To witness duty, not to show my wit :
Duty so great, which wit so poor as mine
May make seem bare, in wanting words to show it,
But that I hope some good conceit of thine
In thy soul's thought, all naked, will bestow it :
Till whatsoever star that guides my moving
Points on me graciously with fair aspect
And puts apparel on my tattered loving
To show me worthy of thy sweet respect :
    Then may I dare to boast how I do love thee,
    Till then not show my head where thou mayst prove me.

26

Lord of my love, whose own merits have much strengthened my sense of duty, I send this token of my service to witness duty, not to vaunt any wit of mine. My wit is indeed bare to express so bounden a duty, but that I hope your good opinion will commend it, all naked as it is, in your inner thoughts, till such time as my fortune takes a more favourable turn and clothes my bare love in such a way as to show me worthy of your respect. Then perhaps I may dare to boast how I love you, will then not show my head where you may prove me.

———

Anyone familiar with Elizabethan usage should realise that the phrase, 'lord of my love', l. 1, is to be taken literally as well as figuratively : the young man to whom the Sonnets are addressed is a lord. It has long been realised how closely the language of this sonnet resembles that of Shakespeare's dedication of *Venus and Adonis* to Southampton : 'I know not how I shall offend in dedicating my unpolished lines to your lordship, nor how the world will censure me for choosing so strong a prop to support so weak a burden : only if your Honour seem but pleased, I account myself highly praised, and vow to take advantage of all idle hours till I have honoured you with some graver labour'.

Throughout the sonnet Shakespeare insists on his duty, the service he owes to his patron ; the tone is one of deep respect from the poet towards one of much superior social station. Ll. 9-12 show that Shakespeare was at this time far from prosperous, and hoped for a better turn to his fortunes. The sestet also shows Shakespeare's hope to justify his patron's confidence with the work he intends, with luck, to achieve. These lines convey a tactful hint to a patron. The sonnet reads like a conclusion, an *envoi* to the whole of this first section, Sonnets 1-26, which may well have formed 'this written ambassage to witness duty' to his lord. The Sonnets are patronage poems written to the patron in course of duty — and so much else besides.

27

Weary with toil, I haste me to my bed,
The dear repose for limbs with travel tired ;
But then begins a journey in my head
To work my mind, when body's work's expired.
For then my thoughts, from far where I abide,
Intend a zealous pilgrimage to thee,
And keep my drooping eyelids open wide,
Looking on darkness which the blind do see :
Save that my soul's imaginary sight
Presents thy shadow to my sightless view,
Which, like a jewel hung in ghastly night,
Makes black night beauteous and her old face new.
  Lo, thus, by day my limbs, by night my mind,
  For thee and for myself no quiet find.

27

Weary with toil, I hurry to my bed, the welcome repose for limbs
tired out with travel; but then, when my body's work is over, I
begin to journey in mind. For my thoughts make pilgrimage to
you, from far away where I am, keeping my drooping eyes wide
open into the dark night where only the blind can see: except that
my imagination brings your shape before me, hung there like a
jewel in the night, making the darkness glow and wear a new face.
Thus, my limbs by day, my mind by night, find no rest for either
of us.

———

This sonnet begins a new series, with Shakespeare journeying away from
proximity to Southampton, into the country. But he finds a new image
for a sonnet to send to his patron — that of the jewel hung in the night.
In *Venus and Adonis* contemporaneously we find the word 'shadow' used
for 'image', as in l. 10 :

> Narcissus so himself himself forsook,
> And died to kiss his shadow in the brook.

We see more clearly that these sonnets are offerings of duty to a patron :
we note Shakespeare's invention labouring to give a new turn to the
well-worn theme, until a new turn in the personal situation, with its
emotional complications, gives fresh inspiration.

The idea that some stones could be seen in the dark is referred to in
Titus Andronicus, II. iii. 226-30 ; while cf. ll. 11-12 with *Romeo and Juliet*,
I. v. 47,

> Her beauty hangs upon the cheek of night
> Like a rich jewel in an Ethiop's ear.

28

How can I then return in happy plight
That am debarred the benefit of rest?
When day's oppression is not eased by night
But day by night, and night by day, oppressed?
And each, though enemies to either's reign,
Do in consent shake hands to torture me,
The one by toil, the other to complain
How far I toil, still farther off from thee.
I tell the day to please him thou art bright
And dost him grace when clouds do blot the heaven:
So flatter I the swart-complexioned night
When sparkling stars twire not thou gild'st the even.
  But day doth daily draw my sorrows longer,
  And night doth nightly make grief's strength seem
    stronger.

28

How can I return in good shape, when I am debarred of the benefit of rest? When the burdens of the day are not eased by night but I am oppressed by both? Both combine to wear me out, one by work, the other by complaining that my work carries me still farther away from you. I assure the day that you are bright to please him and shine even when clouds blot out the sun; I flatter the swarthy night when no star peeps out that you light up the evening. But every day the day draws out my regret, and every night the night makes my grief greater.

———————

We easily perceive that this sonnet was suggested by the previous one and was written as an echo of it. It gives the impression of being a bit jaded : no doubt Shakespeare was tired out, as he complains. However, he manages to make another variation on his theme, even if it sounds artificial. We see in a sonnet like this that such poems were offering of duty. Where was Shakespeare on tour this year? The next sonnet shows that he had no luck. Only the word 'twire' in l. 12 needs explanation : it means to peep.

29

When, in disgrace with fortune and men's eyes,
I all alone beweep my outcast state,
And trouble deaf heaven with my bootless cries,
And look upon myself, and curse my fate :
Wishing me like to one more rich in hope,
Featured like him, like him with friends possessed,
Desiring this man's art and that man's scope,
With what I most enjoy contented least :
Yet in these thoughts myself almost despising,
Haply I think on thee, and then my state,
Like to the lark at break of day arising
From sullen earth, sings hymns at heaven's gate ;
    For thy sweet love remembered such wealth brings
    That then I scorn to change my state with kings.

29

When down on my luck and with people set against me, all alone I lament my lot as an outsider: but I reproach heaven in vain with my laments, when I look upon myself and curse my fate. I wish myself like one with more hope, like him in looks and surrounded with friends; I find myself envying this man's art and that man's range, least contented with what I most enjoy. In this mood almost despising myself, I happen to think of you: and then, like the lark rising at dawn from sullen earth, I chant hymns to heaven. For thinking of your love brings such wealth to mind that then I would not change my state with kings.

———

No artificiality in this famous sonnet : the sincerity shines through ; it is extremely revealing, psychologically and autobiographically. But then we remember Ben Jonson's description of Shakespeare as, above all, 'of an open and free nature'. No disguise about him whatever — and perhaps only a man of the people would have given himself away so freely. We learn more from this about Shakespeare's resentment at the circumstances of his life : these years 1592 and 1593 were a period of extreme discouragement, with the closing of the theatres making it difficult to earn a livelihood — a hazardous existence, as Robert Greene, Watson, Kyd, Peele, Marlowe all found, who all came to an end in these years. And in this year 1592 there came, in addition to the disgrace of fortune, the disgrace in 'men's eyes' of Robert Greene's deathbed attack on him in print, which Shakespeare much resented. The reference in l. 8 —

With what I most enjoy contented least —

would be a reference to his profession as actor. It is not unlikely that, in such moods of depression, he found dissatisfaction in what gave him most pleasure : his acting. Shakespeare is referring to the fortunate young Earl himself in ll. 5–6.

30

When to the sessions of sweet silent thought
I summon up remembrance of things past,
I sigh the lack of many a thing I sought
And with old woes new wail my dear time's waste :
Then can I drown an eye, unused to flow,
For precious friends hid in death's dateless night,
And weep afresh love's long since cancelled woe,
And moan the expense of many a vanished sight :
Then can I grieve at grievances foregone,
And heavily from woe to woe tell o'er
The sad account of fore-bemoanèd moan,
Which I new pay as if not paid before.
   But if the while I think on thee, dear friend,
   All losses are restored and sorrows end.

30

When in these sessions of silent thought I recall memories of past things, I lament the lack of many a thing I wish for and bewail the waste of dear time with old sorrows. Then can I weep, though not so freely now, for beloved friends lost in death's unending night; bewail anew the wounds of former love, regretting what many a vanished sight has cost me. Then can I grieve at past troubles again, and tell over the account of sorrows already grieved for, as if I had not paid the score long ago. But if in this mood I think of you, dear friend, all losses are restored and sorrows brought to an end.

————

The second line of this sonnet has achieved a world-wide circulation in the literature of the twentieth century, with its concern with time. It was taken for an epigraph by Proust for the greatest of modern novels, *A la Recherche du Temps Perdu*. The mood of depression, with absence from his friend, continues and brings back to Shakespeare the thought of earlier friends now dead, and former loves now over.

Observe the alliteration running all through — second nature to a born poet. L. 5, compare the phrase in *Lucrece*, l. 1239, 'they drown their eyes'; l. 6, compare *Romeo and Juliet*, V. iii. 115,

> A dateless bargain to engrossing death.

31

Thy bosom is endearèd with all hearts,
Which I, by lacking, have supposèd dead ;
And there reigns love, and all love's loving parts,
And all those friends which I thought burièd.
How many a holy and obsequious tear
Hath dear religious love stol'n from mine eye,
As interest of the dead, which now appear
But things removed that hidden in thee lie !
Thou art the grave where buried love doth live,
Hung with the trophies of my lovers gone,
Who all their parts of me to thee did give —
That due of many now is thine alone :
    Their images I loved I view in thee,
    And thou, all they, hast all the all of me.

31

You are the dearer to me for all those whom I, missing them, have supposed dead; for love reigns in your breast, and every part of love, and all those friends I thought buried. How many a tear has faithful love stolen from my eye as due to the dead, who now seem to me but absent, lying hidden in you! You are the grave where buried love yet lives, hung with the trophies of my earlier friends, who gave all their share in me to you: what belonged to many now is yours alone: in you I see their loved images, and you, who sum them all up, have all there is of me.

————

Not an easy sonnet of which to follow the train of thought, based as it is on a curious conceit, to us today rather far-fetched. It carries on the thought of the previous sonnet in antiphony : it is a development of it, obviously written at the same time, perhaps on the same day. The theme provides something new to offer the young patron. In l. 5 the word 'obsequious' must be given its literal Elizabethan meaning, *i.e.* pertaining to obsequies.

32

If thou survive my well-contented day
When that churl death my bones with dust shall cover,
And shalt by fortune once more re-survey
These poor rude lines of thy deceasèd lover,
Compare them with the bettering of the time —
And though they be outstripped by every pen,
Reserve them for my love, not for their rhyme,
Exceeded by the height of happier men.
O, then vouchsafe me but this loving thought :
'Had my friend's Muse grown with this growing age,
A dearer birth than this his love had brought,
To march in ranks of better equipage :
   But since he died, and poets better prove,
   Theirs for their style I'll read, his for his love.'

32

If you survive my accepted span, when churlish death has covered
my bones with dust, and by chance read over these poor lines of
your dead friend, comparing them with the progress of the age —
though they may be outstripped by every pen, keep them for my
love, not for their verse, exceeded by the attainments of happier
men. Grant me then but this loving thought: 'had my friend's
muse grown with this improving age, he would have brought a
better offspring than this, to march in better appointed ranks. But
since he died, and poets write better now, I'll read theirs for their
style, his for his love.'

This little-known sonnet tells us much. Shakespeare sees the age as one of
improvement in the art of verse, and it was just in these years that the
sonnet-vogue got going with the publication of Sidney's *Astrophil and
Stella* in 1591, Daniel's *Delia*, and Constable's *Diana* in 1592, Drayton's
Idea in 1593, etc. Shakespeare's Sonnets, however, were unlike anyone
else's: in the fact that they were addressed to a man, for one thing, in
their reality and power, in the openness and intimacy of their confession,
their autobiographical content and the equivocal, tortured story they
proceed to reveal: all this made for their unsuitability for publication,
unlike the other literary sonnet-sequences.

Underneath the self-deprecation one must not miss, with such a
clever man, an element of irony. He knew his own worth.

With the Elizabethans, with their more poetic ways of expression, the
word 'lover' was sometimes used where we should use 'friend'. The
Augustan Malone sagely lays down, 'such addresses to men were
common in Shakespeare's time, and were not thought indecorous'. It
was a recognised expression, rather than a common one, more in place in
verse.

In l. 7, 'reserve them for my love'; this is just what happened: at any
rate, they were reserved, *i.e.* kept, and so we have them.

This concludes the section, Sonnets 27-32, which go together,
evidently written in absence.

33

Full many a glorious morning have I seen
Flatter the mountain-tops with sovereign eye,
Kissing with golden face the meadows green,
Gilding pale streams with heavenly alchemy,
Anon permit the basest clouds to ride
With ugly rack on his celestial face,
And from the forlorn world his visage hide,
Stealing unseen to west with this disgrace.
Even so my sun one early morn did shine
With all-triumphant splendour on my brow ;
But out, alack ! he was but one hour mine,
The region cloud hath masked him from me now.
   Yet him for this my love no whit disdaineth ;
   Suns of the world may stain when heaven's sun staineth.

33

Often have I seen a glorious morning light up the hill-tops, bathe the green meadows in golden sunshine, gilding the pale streams with colour from the skies; and then lowering clouds drive across the sun's face, hiding it from the world, overcast while the sun steals on to the west unseen. Even so my sun one morning shone with splendour on my brow; but then, alas, this was but for an hour: a cloud has masked him from me. Yet love thinks no less of him for this; when the sun in heaven may be overcast, so may the suns in the world beneath.

———

This sonnet announces the first cloud over the friendship, gently enough. The Elizabethans often called the hills of the West Country or the Pennines, mountains. We need not go further than the Cotswolds for the mountain-tops that Shakespeare had often seen touched with the morning sun: they extend a sickle-shaped high ridge to the south and west of Stratford, beyond the meadows and streams that also figure in the picture. Notice the parallel in *The Two Gentlemen of Verona*:

> O, how this spring of love resembleth
> The uncertain glory of an April day,
> Which now shows all the beauty of the sun,
> And by and by a cloud takes all away.

The cloud, as becomes clear, is the young man's breach of trust in responding to the solicitations of Shakespeare's own mistress, Emilia Lanier. This is the inspiration and forms the subject of *The Two Gentlemen*: the competition between the two for the same woman, in which one friend betrays friendship.

34

Why didst thou promise such a beauteous day
And make me travel forth without my cloak,
To let base clouds o'ertake me in my way,
Hiding thy bravery in their rotten smoke ?
'Tis not enough that through the cloud thou break,
To dry the rain on my storm-beaten face,
For no man well of such a salve can speak
That heals the wound and cures not the disgrace :
Nor can thy shame give physic to my grief —
Though thou repent, yet I have still the loss :
The offender's sorrow lends but weak relief
To him that bears the strong offence's cross.
   Ah, but those tears are pearl which thy love sheds,
   And they are rich and ransom all ill deeds.

34

Why did you promise that all was well, so that I took no precaution, and have been caught by this cloud upon our friendship, darkening your looks with suspicion? It's not enough that you should break through the cloud to clear the marks on my storm-beaten face, for no one can think well of a cure that heals the wound but does not remove the disgrace of it. Nor can your shame console my grief — though you repent, I still suffer the consequences: the offender's regret affords little relief to him that bears the heavy cross of the offence. And yet — those tears are pearls when you shed them in love: they richly ransom all ill deeds.

What has happened is that the young man who is so reluctant to marry has been captured by Shakespeare's mistress — the dark woman of the later sonnets. These are not later in time: the story as it unfolds from Sonnets 33 and 34 is duplicated and viewed from the point of view of Shakespeare's relationship to his mistress precisely one hundred sonnets later in the numbering, *i.e.* from 133 onwards. From their place in the sequence this breach of faith would seem to have taken place in Shakespeare's absence. The youth repents in tears and assurance of friendship. All this is borne out by the play, when Proteus (*i.e.* Southampton) says:

> My shame and guilt confounds me.
> Forgive me, Valentine. If hearty sorrow
> Be a sufficient ransom for offence,
> I tender't here. I do as truly suffer
> As e'er I did commit.

To this Valentine (*i.e.* Shakespeare) responds:

> Then I am paid.
> And once again I do receive thee honest.
> Who by repentance is not satisfied
> Is nor of heaven nor earth; for these are pleased.
> By penitence th' Eternal's wrath's appeased.
> And, that my love may appear plain and free,
> All that was mine in Silvia I give thee.

35

No more be grieved at that which thou hast done :
Roses have thorns, and silver fountains mud ;
Clouds and eclipses stain both moon and sun,
And loathsome canker lives in sweetest bud.
All men make faults, and even I in this,
Authorising thy trespass with compare,
Myself corrupting, salving thy amiss,
Excusing thy sins more than thy sins are :
For to thy sensual fault I bring in sense —
Thy adverse party is thy advocate —
And 'gainst myself a lawful plea commence :
Such civil war is in my love and hate,
    That I an accessory needs must be
    To that sweet thief which sourly robs from me.

35

Do not grieve any more at what you have done : roses have thorns, and clear fountains mud. Clouds and eclipses darken both sun and moon, and in the sweetest bud there may be canker. Everybody commits faults, and even I in this, justifying your fault by producing parallels, myself corrupting you by condoning your misdeed, finding more excuse for you than I find offence. For I bring in reason on the side of your sensual fault — your opponent in the case is your advocate — and start a lawful plea against myself : I am so torn in two between love and resentment that I must be an accessory to the loved thief that robs me.

————

Turn to *The Two Gentlemen* and we find Proteus (Southampton) saying:

> Yet writers say, as in the sweetest bud
> The eating canker dwells, so eating love
> Inhabits in the finest wits of all—

i.e. Shakespeare's. To this Valentine (Shakespeare):

> And writers say, as the most forward bud
> Is eaten by the canker ere it blow,
> Even so by love the young and tender wit
> Is turned to folly, blasting in the bud,
> Losing his verdure even in the prime,
> And all the fair effects of future hopes.

Where Shakespeare says 'And writers say', he is referring to himself and what he is writing contemporaneously in the Sonnets, which have the same message for the young man as the play.

36

Let me confess that we two must be twain,
Although our undivided loves are one :
So shall those blots that do with me remain,
Without thy help, by me be borne alone.
In our two loves there is but one respect,
Though in our lives a separable spite,
Which though it alters not love's sole effect,
Yet doth it steal sweet hours from love's delight.
I may not evermore acknowledge thee,
Lest my bewailèd guilt should do thee shame,
Nor thou with public kindness honour me,
Unless thou take that honour from thy name.
　　But do not so : I love thee in such sort
　　As, thou being mine, mine is thy good report.

36

Let me confess that we are divided, though in love we are one; so may those disadvantages I suffer from, without your aid, be borne by me alone. In our loves there is the same regard for each other, though the circumstances of our lives must keep us apart; and though that does not alter the feeling we share, it does take away time from delight in each other's company. I may not always show that I know you in public, lest my own guilt should bring shame on you; nor you honour me with open kindness, lest this detracts from the honour of your name. Do not risk this: my feeling for you is such that, since you are mine, your good name is my chief care.

––––––––

With this breach of trust between them an explanation is necessary: here it is, and it is very revealing. Shakespeare recognises the world of difference there is between their stations, and in the phrase, 'without thy help', l. 4, we may infer that, dependent as he is on Southampton's help in the discouraging circumstances of his life, he is prepared to shoulder them alone. But now, too, Shakespeare has to acknowledge his guilty relations with his mistress, which are publicly known, for he does not wish to besmirch his patron's good name by recognising him, or being recognised, in public. An element of surreptitiousness has entered into their relations : the snake in what was paradise at the beginning.

37

As a decrepit father takes delight
To see his active child do deeds of youth,
So I, made lame by fortune's dearest spite,
Take all my comfort of thy worth and truth ;
For whether beauty, birth, or wealth, or wit,
Or any of these all, or all, or more,
Entitled in thy parts do crownèd sit,
I make my love engrafted to this store :
So then I am not lame, poor, nor despised
Whilst that this shadow doth such substance give
That I in thy abundance am sufficed
And by a part of all thy glory live.
    Look, what is best, that best I wish in thee :
    This wish I have ; then ten times happy me !

37

As a decrepit father takes delight in seeing his child active and
youthful, so I, hampered by ill fortune, derive all my comfort from
your goodness and true heart. Whether beauty or birth, wealth or
wit, or any of them stand out royally among your noble gifts, I
add my love to the store. Then I no longer feel unfortunate, poor
and despised, while this protection gives me such strength that in
your abundance I am content, and live as a part of your glory.
Look, whatever is best, that I wish in and for you: this wish I have,
and in that am ten times blessed.

After the explanation of the previous sonnet, it is natural that there should
be an emotional let-up, and this sonnet describes a more relaxed mood.
There is also a slightly parental note struck at the beginning, which we
have observed before. Notice l. 7 :

> Entitled in thy parts do crownèd sit :

those familiar with the ways of Elizabethan writing will recognise the
oblique reference to the fact that the friend bore a title. The sonnet pro-
vides yet another expression of Shakespeare's resentment at his station, his
ill-fortune in not being independent, his set-backs, slights endured, etc.
The theme runs all through the Sonnets.

38

How can my Muse want subject to invent
While thou dost breathe, that pour'st into my verse
Thine own sweet argument, too excellent
For every vulgar paper to rehearse ?
O, give thyself the thanks, if aught in me
Worthy perusal stand against thy sight ;
For who's so dumb that cannot write to thee,
When thou thyself dost give invention light ?
Be thou the tenth Muse, ten times more in worth
Than those old nine which rhymers invocate ;
And he that calls on thee, let him bring forth
Eternal numbers to outlive long date.
   If my slight Muse do please these curious days,
    The pain be mine, but thine shall be the praise.

38

How can my verse want a subject while you breathe and pour into
my lines yourself, a theme too excellent for vulgar pens? Give
yourself the thanks if anything I have written is worthy your sight;
for who is so dumb as not to be able to write when you inspire?
Let you become the tenth Muse, worth ten times more than the old
nine whom poets invoke; and let him that invokes you bring forth
verse that will live for ever. If my slight Muse please this fastidious
age, let the effort be mine and yours the praise.

———

The relaxed mood continues, but the poem has several points of interest.
It serves to reinforce the view that the Sonnets were written as a regular
part of the poet's service to his patron. It is interesting to have Shake-
speare's view of his age as 'curious', which meant then fastidious, seeking
for novelties. It is not an approving judgment; himself was traditional
and conservative.

39

O, how thy worth with manners may I sing,
When thou art all the better part of me ?
What can mine own praise to mine own self bring ?
And what is't but mine own when I praise thee ?
Even for this let us divided live,
And our dear love lose name of single one,
That by this separation I may give
That due to thee which thou deserv'st alone.
O absence, what a torment wouldst thou prove
Were it not thy sour leisure gave sweet leave
To entertain the time with thoughts of love,
Which time and thoughts so sweetly doth deceive,
  And that thou teachest how to make one twain
  By praising him here who doth hence remain.

39

How can I with modesty praise your worth, when you are the better part of me ? What can my own praises award myself, and what is it but my own when I praise you ? Let us live divided, then, and our love forego its singleness, that by this separation I may give you that due which you deserve alone. What a torment absence would be did it not give leisure to occupy the time with thoughts of love, beguiling both time and thoughts, and if it did not teach how to make one into two by praising him here who in fact is absent.

———————

In this Shakespeare contrives yet another ingenious variation, evidently written in absence. Southampton is away; once more Shakespeare accepts their inevitable separateness. L. 11 has become so familiar as to be almost proverbial; it has a parallel in *Lucrece*, l. 1361:

The weary time she cannot entertain.

40

Take all my loves, my love, yea, take them all :
What hast thou then more than thou hadst before ?
No love, my love, that thou mayst true love call ;
All mine was thine before thou hadst this more.
Then, if for my love thou my love receivest,
I cannot blame thee for my love thou usest ;
But yet be blamed, if thou this self deceivest
By wilful taste of what thyself refusest.
I do forgive thy robbery, gentle thief,
Although thou steal thee all my poverty ;
And yet, love knows, it is a greater grief
To bear love's wrong than hate's known injury.
    Lascivious grace, in whom all ill well shows,
    Kill me with spites, yet we must not be foes.

40

Take all my loves, take them all : what have you got more than you
had before ? Nothing, my dearest, that may be called true love ;
all mine was yours before you had this in addition. Then, if you
take to yourself my lover out of love for me, I cannot blame you
for using her ; and yet you may be blamed, if you deceive me by
wilfully tasting what you refuse lawfully. I forgive your robbery,
though you steal all I have ; yet, love knows it is harder to bear the
wrong love does than the injury of hate. Lascivious grace, in
whom even ill shows attractive, injure me as you will, so long as
we do not become enemies.

———————

This important sonnet offers some difficulty, the situation is so equivocal
beneath the polite language of conceit. The young patron has taken his
poet's mistress — though Shakespeare does not call that relation 'true
love'. Shakespeare does not reproach him for taking her, but for taking
her while himself refusing to marry. There is an implied reproach, too, in
the young lord taking from his poet's poverty. But what are we to make
of l. 5 ? —

Then, if for my love thou my love receivest.

Southampton became acquainted with the lady through writing to her
on Shakespeare's behalf. But what could Shakespeare have done about it,
in his situation of dependence? He evidently decided to make the best of
it. Not very dignified; but, then, he was not in a position to stand on his
dignity.

41

Those pretty wrongs that liberty commits,
When I am sometime absent from thy heart,
Thy beauty and thy years full well befits,
For still temptation follows where thou art.
Gentle thou art, and therefore to be won,
Beauteous thou art, therefore to be assailed.
And when a woman woos, what woman's son
Will sourly leave her till she have prevailed?
Ay me! but yet thou mightst my seat forbear,
And chide thy beauty and thy straying youth,
Who lead thee in their riot even there
Where thou art forced to break a twofold truth:
   Hers, by thy beauty tempting her to thee,
   Thine, by thy beauty being false to me.

41

Those little wrongs you are at liberty to commit when I am sometimes absent from your heart, befit your youth and beauty, for temptation follows you wherever you are. You are gentle, and therefore to be won; handsome, and therefore to be tried. And when a woman woos, what woman's son will leave her till she has had her way? Yet, alas, you might forbear to take my place, and restrain your erring youth that leads you to where you are forced to make a double breach of faith: hers, tempted by your good looks; yours, in being false to me.

————

This sonnet, after the covert language of the preceding one, makes the situation quite explicit: the poet's mistress is after the young lord, and he is willing. Shakespeare needed all his tact to support it, and tact of expression to express it. The reproach is expressed in terms of praise. Needs must ; but the subtlety lies in that it is also genuine.

Ll. 7-8 : notice the closeness to *Venus and Adonis*, ll. 201-2 :

> Art thou a woman's son and canst not feel
> What 'tis to love, how want of love tormenteth ?

42

That thou hast her it is not all my grief,
And yet it may be said I loved her dearly ;
That she hath thee is of my wailing chief,
A loss in love that touches me more nearly.
Loving offenders, thus I will excuse ye :
Thou dost love her, because thou know'st I love her ;
And for my sake even so doth she abuse me,
Suffering my friend for my sake to approve her.
If I lose thee, my loss is my love's gain,
And losing her, my friend hath found that loss :
Both find each other, and I lose both twain,
And both for my sake lay on me this cross.
    But here's the joy : my friend and I are one ;
    Sweet flattery ! then she loves but me alone.

42

It is not my main ground of complaint that you have her, even though I loved her dearly ; that she has you is my chief regret, a loss that touches me more closely. Loving offenders, I excuse you thus : you love her, because you know I love her ; similarly she abuses me for my sake, in allowing my friend to try her. If I lose you, my loss is a gain to my love ; and losing her, my friend picks up the loss. Both find each other, I lose both, and both lay this cross on me for my sake. But there is consolation in this thought : my friend and I are one, therefore she loves but me alone.

———

It says something for the resources of poetry, and the resilience of the poet, to be able to go on making variations in this complication of the theme. Shakespeare has to content himself with a poor consolation at the end, but 'beggars can't be choosers'. The sonnet is an *envoi* to the section 33-42. The subject of the imbroglio, the triangular relationship, is taken up more fully and treated more seriously in the Dark Lady sequence, Sonnet 127 foll., from the different angle of Shakespeare's relations with her.

43

When most I wink then do mine eyes best see,
For all the day they view things unrespected ;
But when I sleep, in dreams they look on thee,
And, darkly bright, are bright in dark directed.
And thou, whose shadow shadows doth make bright,
How would thy shadow's form form happy show
To the clear day with thy much clearer light,
When to unseeing eyes thy shade shines so !
How would, I say, mine eyes be blessèd made
By looking on thee in the living day,
When in dead night thy fair imperfect shade
Through heavy sleep on sightless eyes doth stay !
    All days are nights to see till I see thee,
    And nights bright days when dreams do show thee me.

43

When most I close my eyes then do I see best, for all day I look at things I do not care for; but sleeping I see you in dreams: my eyes, darkly bright, are clearly directed in the dark. And you, whose image makes darkness bright, how would your form itself show happy in clear daylight when to closed eyes your shade shines so! How blessed should I be to look on you in the living day, when in the dead of night your shadow is imprinted on closed eyes in sleep! All days are like dark nights till I see you, and nights like bright days when dreams reveal you to me.

This sonnet starts a new series written in absence. That this is written in duty is obvious. Shakespeare is repeating himself, cf. Sonnet 27.

44

If the dull substance of my flesh were thought,
Injurious distance should not stop my way ;
For then, despite of space, I would be brought,
From limits far remote where thou dost stay.
No matter then although my foot did stand
Upon the farthest earth removed from thee ;
For nimble thought can jump both sea and land,
As soon as think the place where he would be.
But, ah ! thought kills me that I am not thought,
To leap large lengths of miles when thou art gone,
But that, so much of earth and water wrought,
I must attend time's leisure with my moan ;
    Receiving nought by elements so slow
    But heavy tears, badges of either's woe.

44

If only the heavy substance of my body were turned into thought, the disadvantage of distance would not be in my way; for then, in spite of space, I should be brought from far away to where you are. It would not matter whether I were at the farthest limit of earth from you, for swift thought can jump sea and land as soon as think where one would be. Alas, it kills me to think that I am not thought, to leap over the long miles between us, but that, being made so much of the heavier elements, I must await time's leisure, receiving from these nothing but heavy tears, emblems of each other's grief.

————

The thought of this sonnet is not altogether easy ; the idea it plays with is that of the two heavy elements, earth and water, according to Elizabethan science ; the two light elements being air and fire. Of these was the universe supposed to be composed. The situation is that Southampton is absent as usual.

45

The other two, slight air and purging fire,
Are both with thee, wherever I abide :
The first my thought, the other my desire,
These present-absent with swift motion slide.
For when these quicker elements are gone
In tender embassy of love to thee,
My life, being made of four, with two alone
Sinks down to death, oppressed with melancholy.
Until life's composition be recured
By those swift messengers returned from thee,
Who even but now come back again, assured
Of thy fair health, recounting it to me :
    This told, I joy ; but then no longer glad,
    I send them back again, and straight grow sad.

45

The other two elements, air and fire, are with you, wherever I am :
the first is my thought, the second my desire, these swiftly inter-
changing presence with absence. When these lighter elements are
gone on embassy to you, my life, being made of four, sinks down
to heaviness and melancholy. Until the proper composition of
life is recovered by those swift messengers returned from you, who
even at this moment come back, assuring me of your good health.
Hearing this, I am happy ; and then, sending back thought and
desire to you again, I am left sad.

This continues and completes the thought of Sonnet 44: the two go
together, composed together in absence, as offerings of duty. We notice
how often the sonnets go in pairs, the thought or conceit of one being
complemented or returned in a second, antiphonally. A good way of
spinning out poems to meet requirements.

46

Mine eye and heart are at a mortal war
How to divide the conquest of thy sight :
Mine eye, my heart thy picture's sight would bar,
My heart, mine eye the freedom of that right.
My heart doth plead that thou in him dost lie —
A closet never pierced with crystal eyes —
But the defendant doth that plea deny,
And says in him thy fair appearance lies.
To 'cide this title is impanellèd
A quest of thoughts, all tenants to the heart,
And by their verdict is determinèd
The clear eye's moiety and the dear heart's part :
   As thus : mine eye's due is thine outward part,
   And my heart's right thine inward love of heart.

46

My eye and heart are in conflict how to divide the conquest of your image. The eye would debar the heart of the sight of your picture, the heart deny the eye any such liberty. The heart pleads that you lie there — a closet never pierced by mortal eyes; but the defendant denies this and claims that your appearance lies in him. To decide this a jury of thoughts is impanelled — all of them the heart's tenants — and their verdict determines the issue between eye and heart. In this wise: your outward part is the eye's due, your inner heart's love is my heart's right.

———

Never was there more obviously a duty-sonnet: all too ingenious and unmoving to our taste. However, Elizabethan taste was another matter. Contemporary life is reflected in the image of impanelling the jury, the tenants of the manor: their verdict was to award a 'moiety', l. 12, *i.e.* one-half, to each. We still retain the word 'quest' in local country speech: a 'crowner's quest' means coroner's inquest.

47

Betwixt mine eye and heart a league is took,
And each doth good turns now unto the other :
When that mine eye is famished for a look,
Or heart in love with sighs himself doth smother,
With my love's picture then my eye doth feast,
And to the painted banquet bids my heart ;
Another time mine eye is my heart's guest
And in his thoughts of love doth share a part.
So, either by thy picture or my love,
Thyself away art present still with me ;
For thou not farther than my thoughts canst move,
And I am still with them and they with thee.
  Or, if they sleep, thy picture in my sight
  Awakes my heart to heart's and eye's delight.

47

A league is made between eye and heart, and now each does good turns to the other : when my eye is famished for a look or my heart smothered in sighs, the one feasts on my love's picture and bids the heart to that painted feast ; another time the eye is the heart's guest and shares in its thoughts of love. So, either by your picture or my love, you are still present with me when away ; for you are not farther than my thoughts can move, and I am ever with them as they are with you. Or, if they are asleep, your picture in my sight awakes both eye and heart to pleasure.

———

This continues the thought of the previous poem, and is its antiphon, or chime. We may infer from it that Southampton had given his poet a picture of himself — perhaps a miniature, which Shakespeare carried with him in his absence. L. 3 is closely paralleled in *The Comedy of Errors*, II. i. 88 :

Whilst I at home starve for a merry look.

48

How careful was I, when I took my way,
Each trifle under truest bars to thrust,
That to my use it might unusèd stay
From hands of falsehood, in sure wards of trust !
But thou, to whom my jewels trifles are,
Most worthy comfort, now my greatest grief,
Thou best of dearest and mine only care,
Art left the prey of every vulgar thief.
Thee have I not locked up in any chest,
Save where thou art not, though I feel thou art,
Within the gentle closure of my breast,
From whence at pleasure thou mayst come and part ;
   And even thence thou wilt be stol'n, I fear,
   For truth proves thievish for a prize so dear.

48

How careful I was, when I went away, to put every trifle under lock
and key that it might remain shut up safely, untouched by thievish
hands. But you, to whom my trinkets are but trifles — my dearest
comfort and now my chief concern, my fondest love and only care
— are left the prey of every common thief. I have not been able to
lock you up in any chest, save where you are not — though I feel
you are — within my breast, whence you may come and go as you
will. And I fear you will be stolen even from there, for honesty
itself turns thief for so dear a prize.

Suggestive autobiographically ; we see Shakespeare, on leaving his room
in London, locking up his few possessions. But he cannot put the young
lord under lock and key: he remains there, a prey to any who attempt
him. We hear the accents of apprehension and mistrust, for the young
man, during Shakespeare's absence, is the object of his mistress's atten-
tions. The latter receives a kind, if oblique, compliment in the last line,
'for truth proves thievish' : we shall see how true she was. On the
other hand, there is Shakespeare's intense and intimate concern for South-
ampton : 'thou best of dearest and mine only care'. (What about the
family at Stratford ? Well, Shakespeare was doing his best to maintain
them. His relation to his patron was part of that too.) How complex
it has all become, in the manner of such things, after the simplicity of the
beginning ! Again we note a certain protective, quasi-parental feeling
on the part of the poet.
    L. 4 : we still use the word 'wards', though rarely : it means the
notches on key and lock that fit each other.

49

Against that time, if ever that time come,
When I shall see thee frown on my defects,
When as thy love hath cast his utmost sum,
Called to that audit by advised respects :
Against that time when thou shalt strangely pass,
And scarcely greet me with that sun, thine eye,
When love, converted from the thing it was,
Shall reasons find of settled gravity :
Against that time do I ensconce me here
Within the knowledge of mine own desert,
And this my hand against myself uprear,
To guard the lawful reasons on thy part :
    To leave poor me thou hast the strength of laws,
    Since why to love I can allege no cause.

49

Against the time, if ever it comes, when I shall see you frown on my failings, when your love closes its account, arrived at on careful consideration of circumstances : against the time when you will pass me like a stranger, scarcely seeing me, when love has ceased to be what it was and has to find sufficient reasons for it: against that time I fortify myself in the knowledge of what I deserve, and raise my own hand against myself to witness your right to disown me. You have every right to leave poor me, since there is no reason why you should love me.

There is no mistaking the accents of sincerity in this fine sonnet. Sadness chimes throughout it in the thrice repeated 'against that time' ; but there is also the psychological prevision of the inevitable, and — what is so characteristic of Shakespeare — the acceptance. There is no illusion about the relationship between the proud young lord and the poet whom he is pleased to favour, between the handsome youth and the older man, who accepts the inevitability of 'that time when thou shalt strangely pass and scarcely greet me'. Years later, in *Julius Caesar*, IV. ii. 21, there is a reflection of this:

> When love begins to sicken and decay,
> It useth an enforcèd ceremony.

At the same time, the figures used are those of an account, the last sum in the audit, raising one's hand in a court of law as witness, being left poor. There is the reminder, so tactfully put, of the poet's dependence on his patron : reverse 'poor me', in l. 13, to read 'to leave me poor', and one gets the hint.

Observe, in this awkward situation, Shakespeare's characteristic grand language, the tactful abstractness of 'advised respects', 'reasons find of settled gravity'.

50

How heavy do I journey on the way
When what I seek, my weary travel's end,
Doth teach that ease and that repose to say,
'Thus far the miles are measured from thy friend.'
The beast that bears me, tired with my woe,
Plods dully on, to bear that weight in me,
As if by some instinct the wretch did know
His rider loved not speed, being made from thee :
The bloody spur cannot provoke him on
That sometimes anger thrusts into his hide,
Which heavily he answers with a groan,
More sharp to me than spurring to his side ;
   For that same groan doth put this in my mind :
   My grief lies onward, and my joy behind.

50

How heavily I jog on my way, when what I seek — my weary journey's end — speaks to me, when I reach my repose, only of the miles that I have measured away from my friend. The poor beast that bears me — sick at heart — plods dully on, as if by some instinct he knows that his rider does not want speed, since it takes him away from you. Even the spur does not drive him on, when sometimes impatiently I thrust it into his side : he answers with a groan that pierces me more than the spur does him — for it puts me in mind that my grief lies before me, my happiness behind.

––––––––––

After the psychological complexity of the previous sonnet, we are grateful for the simplicity of this : a picture of Shakespeare journeying on his horse into the country, away from London and his patron, probably on tour, or perhaps going home to Stratford.

51

Thus can my love excuse the slow offence
Of my dull bearer, when from thee I speed :
From where thou art, why should I haste me thence ?
Till I return, of posting is no need.
O, what excuse will my poor beast then find,
When swift extremity can seem but slow ?
Then should I spur, though mounted on the wind,
In wingèd speed no motion shall I know :
Then can no horse with my desire keep pace.
Therefore desire, of perfect'st love being made,
Shall neigh, no dull flesh, in his fiery race ;
But love, for love, thus shall excuse my jade :
   Since from thee going he went wilful-slow,
   Towards thee I'll run and give him leave to go.

51

Thus can my love excuse the slowness of my horse in going from you : from where you are, why should I haste away ? Until I return, there is no need of hurrying. But what excuse will my poor beast find then, when the fastest speed will seem slow to me ? Then I should spur, if I were mounted on the wind, nor even feel any motion however swift : no horse could keep pace with my desire. Therefore desire, being made of the most perfect love, shall cry out — no mere flesh — in a fiery race. Love, in return for love, shall excuse my steed : since going away from you he went wilfully slow, in returning I shall race and let him walk.

———

The companion-piece to Sonnet 50, rather laboured to our taste. A duty-piece, though the feeling is genuine enough : it is a little difficult to follow the thought of ll. 11-12. It is more pleasing to reflect that Shakespeare was a good judge of horse-flesh, and had a fellow-feeling for his poor beast of burden.

52

So am I as the rich, whose blessèd key
Can bring him to his sweet up-lockèd treasure,
The which he will not every hour survey,
For blunting the fine point of seldom pleasure.
Therefore are feasts so solemn and so rare
Since, seldom coming, in the long year set,
Like stones of worth they thinly placèd are,
Or captain jewels in the carcanet.
So is the time that keeps you as my chest,
Or as the wardrobe which the robe doth hide,
To make some special instant special blest,
By new unfolding his imprisoned pride.
    Blessèd are you, whose worthiness gives scope,
      Being had — to triumph, being lacked — to hope.

52

Thus am I like a rich man, whose key can open to him his locked-up treasure, which he is not for ever looking at, lest he should lose the exquisite pleasure by enjoying it too often. Therefore are feasts so rare and cherished, since, coming seldom in the year, they are spaced out like the finest jewels in a necklace. So time operates that keeps you as my chest, or as a wardrobe concealing the robe, to make some special moment specially blessed, unfolding it to reveal the sight of you withheld from me. Thus are you blessed, whose worth has such power that in your presence I triumph, in absence I hope.

———

How ingenious ! this reminds us again how clever a writer, apart from anything else, Shakespeare was ; with what ease he wrote these endless variations on his theme. This goes back to the theme of Sonnet 48, of the poet's locked chest with its few possessions, and the key. There is the extraordinary ease and conciseness of such a line as l. 4, impossible to render as pointedly in prose. It is clear that Shakespeare saw his patron only at intervals.

53

What is your substance, whereof are you made,
That millions of strange shadows on you tend ?
Since every one hath, every one, one shade,
And you, but one, can every shadow lend.
Describe Adonis, and the counterfeit
Is poorly imitated after you ;
On Helen's cheek all art of beauty set,
And you in Grecian tires are painted new :
Speak of the spring and foison of the year,
The one doth shadow of your beauty show,
The other as your bounty doth appear ;
And you in every blessèd shape we know.
   In all external grace you have some part,
   But you like none, none you, for constant heart.

53

Of what substance are you made, that innumerable shadows attend on you ? Everyone has but one shadow, yet you — only one person — can cast every shadow. Describe Adonis, and the description is a poor imitation of you ; set out Helen in all her beauty, and you appear anew in Grecian guise. Speak of spring and harvest : the one is the shadow of your beauty, as the other is of your bounty : we recognise you in every good shape we know. In all external graces you have some share, but there is none like you for a constant heart.

———

From the relaxed ease of this, the sense of gratitude, the emphasis on Southampton's generosity of heart, I think we may infer that the poet had been the recipient of his patron's bounty. There is less anxiety in these sonnets. At this time Adonis, ll. 5-6, was much in mind, for Shakespeare was writing *Venus and Adonis* for his young patron, describing him in it recognisably as Adonis. The comparison with Helen reminds us of Sonnet 20 and the description of Southampton as combining the best of both masculine and feminine attractions. This was very much a Renaissance theme, as in the court-poems addressed to Henri III.

54

O, how much more doth beauty beauteous seem
By that sweet ornament which truth doth give !
The rose looks fair, but fairer we it deem
For that sweet odour which doth in it live.
The canker-blooms have full as deep a dye
As the perfumèd tincture of the roses,
Hang on such thorns, and play as wantonly
When summer's breath their maskèd buds discloses :
But, for their virtue only is their show,
They live unwooed and unrespected fade,
Die to themselves. Sweet roses do not so :
Of their sweet deaths are sweetest odours made :
   And so of you, beauteous and lovely youth,
   When that shall fade, my verse distils your truth.

54

How much more admirable is beauty when the ornament of truth is added to it! The rose looks fair, but we think more highly of it for the fragrance it has. Scentless wild roses have as good a colour as the scented rose, flower on such thorns, and play as prettily in the summer breeze that opens their buds. But their only merit is their show : we do not pluck them and they fade unregarded, die on their own. With scented roses it is not so : they perish to create sweet essences. And so of you, lovely youth, when that fades, my verse will distil your quality.

In the sonnets of this section one has the impression of anxiety relaxed, a sense of gratitude : which Shakespeare repays by promising his patron immortality in his verse. The promise was fulfilled. L. 12, 'Of their sweet deaths are sweetest odours made' : it is touching to hear the echo of this, years later, towards the end of Shakespeare's life, in *The Tempest* : 'Of his bones are coral made'.

statues

sun - son

55

Not marble, nor the gilded monuments
Of princes, shall outlive this powerful rhyme;
But you shall shine more bright in these contents
Than unswept stone, besmeared with sluttish time.
god of war
When wasteful war shall statues overturn,
And broils root out the work of masonry,
Nor Mars's sword nor war's quick fire shall burn
The living record of your memory.
'Gainst death and all-oblivious enmity _always_
Shall you pace forth : your praise shall still find room
Even in the eyes of all posterity — _future generations_
That wear this world out to the ending doom.
So, till the judgment that yourself arise,
You live in this, and dwell in lovers' eyes.

discussing different memorials

_defeating time in memory
until judgement day the words
of his sonnet will be passed on._

Time - infinite, enemy, weapon, ageing

love death preservation

art

112

55

_{wealthy, powerful people}

Neither marble nor princes' gilded monuments shall outlive these verses: you shall shine more bright in them than unswept stone, dirty with decay.   When wasteful war shall overturn statues and throw down buildings, neither sword nor fire shall destroy the living record of your memory.   Against death and injurious oblivion shall you go forward: your praise shall still find place even in the eyes of posterity, until doomsday ends the world.   So, till the day of judgment calls you to arise, you will live on in this and in the eyes of lovers.

———

All that one can say about this famous sonnet, this splendid incantation, is to notice the outburst of confidence in his verse on the part of the poet. Perhaps it came, naturally enough, along with the relief of his anxiety. Nor was he wrong: wars have come and gone, London been twice burnt down, yet Shakespeare's friend goes on immortally in his verse, as the poet assured him.

56

Sweet love, renew thy force : be it not said
Thy edge should blunter be than appetite,
Which but today by feeding is allayed,
Tomorrow sharpened in his former might.
So, love, be thou : although today thou fill
Thy hungry eyes even till they wink with fulness,
Tomorrow see again, and do not kill
The spirit of love with a perpetual dulness.
Let this sad interim like the ocean be
Which parts the shore, where two contracted new
Come daily to the banks, that when they see
Return of love, more blest may be the view.
    Or call it winter, which, being full of care,
      Makes summer's welcome thrice more wished, more
        rare.

56

Love, renew your power: let it not be weaker than desire, which today is satisfied but tomorrow is revived as strong as before. So, love, with you: although today you fill your hungry eyes till they close satiated, tomorrow open them wide again: do not allow the spirit of love to sink into drowsiness. Let this sad interval be like the sea parting the shore, where two betrothed lovers come daily to the sea-side, to see a view made happier by the return of love. Or like winter, which, being full of care, makes the arrival of summer all the more rare and desirable.

It is a little difficult to be sure of the situation here : there is a certain feeling of drifting apart in the poem. What does 'sad interim', l. 9, imply? I do not think it is merely absence. The poet would seem to be whipping up the young man's flagging affection. Behind ll. 9-12 flickers a reminiscence of the situation of Hero and Leander.

57

Being your slave, what should I do but tend
Upon the hours and times of your desire ?
I have no precious time at all to spend,
Nor services to do, till you require.
Nor dare I chide the world-without-end hour
Whilst I, my sovereign, watch the clock for you,
Nor think the bitterness of absence sour
When you have bid your servant once adieu.
Nor dare I question with my jealous thought
Where you may be, or your affairs suppose,
But like a sad slave stay and think of nought
Save, where you are, how happy you make those.
 So true a fool is love that in your will,
 Though you do anything, he thinks no ill.

57

Being your slave, what should I do but wait upon the timing of your wishes? I have nothing to do with my time, no services to perform, till you command. Nor do I complain of the tedious hours while I watch the clock for you, my lord and master, nor think absence bitter when you have bidden your servant adieu. Nor dare I question jealously where you may be, or what you may be doing, but sadly wait and think of nothing but that, with whomever you may be, you make them happy. So devoted a fool is love that whatever you wish or do, he thinks no ill.

———

This takes us into the reality of the situation. One sees the picture: the spoiled young peer, with his lordly ways, keeping the older man, his poet and servant, waiting on his pleasure. One sees Shakespeare kept waiting, while his lord is elsewhere, out and about. Shakespeare's time does not matter; it is his to wait on his young master. Underneath the sad dignity of the polite phrasing, one recognises the accents of reproach and of a gentle irony. L. 13 has a play on the word 'will', emphasised in the original with a capital, 'Will', for Shakespeare himself.

58

That God forbid, that made me first your slave,
I should in thought control your times of pleasure,
Or at your hand the account of hours to crave,
Being your vassal, bound to stay your leisure.
O let me suffer, being at your beck,
The imprisoned absence of your liberty,
And patience tame to sufferance, bide each check,
Without accusing you of injury.
Be where you list, your charter is so strong
That you yourself may privilege your time
To what you will, to you it doth belong
Yourself to pardon of self-doing crime.
   I am to wait, though waiting so be hell,
   Not blame your pleasure, be it ill or well.

58

God, who first made me your slave, forbid that I should even in thought control your times of pleasure, or seek to know how you spend your hours — since I am your servant, bound to await your leisure. Being at your beck and call, let me suffer your absence, while you are free to roam, tame patience into endurance, bide every rebuke without accusing you of injury. Wherever you may be, your liberty is so entire that you may occupy your time as you will : it is your prerogative to pardon yourself of any ill you may do yourself. I am to wait, though waiting may be hell, not blame your pleasure whether good or ill.

———

The reproach is strengthened in this — and how well one recognises the situation : the older man is left to kick his heels, while the younger is off on his own. Shakespeare does not pry into what he is up to, though the impression left by the sonnet is that he is up to no good. Shakespeare recognises with his half-ironic humility, though there is reproach in the recognition — that he is Southampton's servant and has no right to expect an account of how he spends his time, though the implication of 'self-doing crime', l. 12, is that he is doing himself harm. Here again is Shakespeare's characteristic double-mindedness : there is a tutorial solicitude in the dependant's reproach.

59

If there be nothing new, but that which is
Hath been before, how are our brains beguiled,
Which, labouring for invention, bear amiss
The second burden of a former child !
O, that record could with a backward look,
Even of five hundred courses of the sun,
Show me your image in some antique book,
Since mind at first in character was done.
That I might see what the old world could say
To this composèd wonder of your frame,
Whether we are mended, or where better they,
Or whether revolution be the same.
   O, sure I am, the wits of former days
   To subjects worse have given admiring praise.

59

If there is nothing new in the world, but that which is has been before, how are our brains cheated, which — seeking to create something new — bring forth something already in existence ! O, that memory could look back five hundred years to show me your picture in some ancient book, since thought was first expressed in writing. So that I might see what an earlier world could say to this perfection of your frame : whether we have improved or they were better, or whether the cycle of years has brought us to the same point. Of one thing I am sure : the wits of former days have given praise to much worse subjects.

This curious and little-quoted sonnet yet tells us something about Shakespeare's attitude to his writing, and his own situation in turning out these poems. L. 3, 'labouring for invention', shows his determination to write something new. The suggestion at the back of this poem may well come from *Ecclesiastes*, i. 9 foll., 'The thing that hath been, it is that which shall be ; and that which is done is that which shall be done : and there is no new thing under the sun'.

60

Like as the waves make towards the pebbled shore
So do our minutes hasten to their end ;
Each changing place with that which goes before
In sequent toil all forwards do contend.
Nativity, once in the main of light,
Crawls to maturity, wherewith being crowned
Crooked eclipses 'gainst his glory fight,
And time that gave doth now his gift confound.
Time doth transfix the flourish set on youth
And delves the parallels in beauty's brow,
Feeds on the rarities of nature's truth,
And nothing stands but for his scythe to mow :
   And yet to times in hope my verse shall stand,
   Praising thy worth, despite his cruel hand.

60

Just as the waves make towards the pebbly shore, so our minutes hasten onwards to their end ; each following the one before, they move forward in sequence. Nativity, once in the centre of light, crawls on to maturity — which, being achieved, suffers eclipse and frustration, and time that gave now takes away. Time destroys the bloom of youth and traces lines in the brow, feeds on nature's rarities, and nothing stands but for his scythe to mow down. Yet my verse in praise of you shall stand to future times, in spite of time's cruelty.

———

Evidently a duty-sonnet, rather conventional. The first quatrain closely follows Golding's translation of Ovid's *Metamorphoses*, XV. 201-3 :

> As every wave drives other forth
>   and that that comes behind
> Both thrusteth and is thrust itself :
>   Even so the times by kind
> Do fly and follow both at once,
>   and evermore renew.

Behold, however, the contrast between ordinary Elizabethan jog-trot and Shakespeare !

61

Is it thy will thy image should keep open
My heavy eyelids to the weary night ?
Dost thou desire my slumbers should be broken,
While shadows like to thee do mock my sight ?
Is it thy spirit that thou send'st from thee
So far from home into my deeds to pry,
To find out shames and idle hours in me,
The scope and tenure of thy jealousy ?
O no, thy love, though much, is not so great :
It is my love that keeps mine eye awake,
Mine own true love that doth my rest defeat
To play the watchman ever for thy sake.
   For thee watch I, whilst thou dost wake elsewhere,
   From me far off, with others all too near.

61

Is it your will that your image should keep me wakeful at night, that my sleep should be broken while shades of you haunt my sight ? Is it your spirit that you send so far from home to pry into my deeds, to see how ill I spend my time — the aim and scope of your suspicion ? No, your love is not so strong : it is my love that keeps me awake, my own true love that cheats me of my rest to play the watchman over you. I keep watch for you, while you are awake elsewhere, far off from me, with others all too near.

———

Here are the accents of sincerity, depicting a situation all too familiar : the disparity in love, as well as circumstances and fortune, between the older and the younger man. Notice in l. 7 the 'idle hours', the phrase that appears again in the dedication of *Venus and Adonis* to Southampton in 1593 : 'I vow to take advantage of all idle hours, till I have honoured you with some graver labour'.

62

Sin of self-love possesseth all mine eye,
And all my soul, and all my every part ;
And for this sin there is no remedy,
It is so grounded inward in my heart.
Methinks no face so gracious is as mine,
No shape so true, no truth of such account ;
And for myself mine own worth do define
As I all others in all worths surmount.
But when my glass shows me myself indeed,
Beated and chopped with tanned antiquity,
Mine own self-love quite contrary I read :
Self, so self-loving, were iniquity.
  'Tis thee, myself, that for myself I praise,
  Painting my age with beauty of thy days.

62

Sin of self-love possesses my eye, my soul, and every part of me;
there is no remedy for it, it is so grounded inwardly in my heart. I
think no face more charming, no one more upright, no one so
dependable; in my own valuation I surpass all others. But when
my mirror shows me myself as I am, storm-beaten and chapped
with the years, I read the contradiction of any vanity: it were
iniquitous to love the self I see. It is you, my other self, that I praise
in myself, disguising my age with your youth and beauty.

In spite of the ingenious conceit upon which the poem is based, it is a
natural movement of the mind from the theme of disparity in love to
the disillusionment in this — all the more pathetic for being a compli-
ment to the youthful patron in the form of undressing the older man's
vanity. However, it provides a theme for another sonnet for the patron
— and a curious one psychologically; for Shakespeare was modest enough
yet had a good opinion of himself. L. 4 reflects the Prayer Book phrase,
'grafted inwardly in our hearts', which he heard in church all his days.
As for ll. 5-6, we recall Aubrey : 'He was a handsome, well-shaped man :
very good company, and of a very ready and pleasant smooth wit'.
Brief Lives, ed. A. Clark, vol. II, p. 226.

63

Against my love shall be, as I am now,
With Time's injurious hand crushed and o'er-worn ;
When hours have drained his blood and filled his brow
With lines and wrinkles ; when his youthful morn
Hath travelled on to age's steepy night,
And all those beauties whereof now he's king
Are vanishing or vanished out of sight,
Stealing away the treasure of his spring :
For such a time do I now fortify
Against confounding age's cruel knife,
That he shall never cut from memory
My sweet love's beauty, though my lover's life :
 His beauty shall in these black lines be seen,
 And they shall live, and he in them still green.

63

Against the time when my love shall be, as I am now, worn by time, when the years have drained his blood and filled his brow with lines; when the morning of youth has moved on to the night of age, and all the charms he now commands are vanishing or vanished out of sight, the treasure of his spring consumed: for such a time do I take measures against the cruel edge of age, that it may never cut from memory my love's beauty, though it may my lover's life: his beauty shall live on in these black lines, and they will keep his memory green.

Such a relationship was bound to bring out Shakespeare's consciousness of how much older he was than the young man — practically a decade, and that meant much more then than now : the poet's life was more than half over. No doubt he had worn hard — cf. 'o'er worn', l. 2 — with his long struggle to establish himself and with his way of life. All the same, the emphasis on his age is an implied compliment to the youth of his patron. L. 5 : 'age's steepy night' refers to the course and decline of the sun in the sky.

64

When I have seen by Time's fell hand defaced
The rich, proud cost of outworn buried age ;
When sometime lofty towers I see down-razed,
And brass eternal slave to mortal rage ;
When I have seen the hungry ocean gain
Advantage on the kingdom of the shore,
And the firm soil win of the watery main,
Increasing store with loss and loss with store ;
When I have seen such interchange of state,
Or state itself confounded to decay,
Ruin hath taught me thus to ruminate,
That Time will come and take my love away.
   This thought is as a death, which cannot choose
   But weep to have that which it fears to lose.

64

When I have seen the proud monuments of the gorgeous past defaced by time, lofty towers thrown down and brasses laid for eternity ripped up by men's fury; when I have seen the hungry sea eating away the shore, or the land gaining upon the sea, alternating loss with gain ; when I have seen such changes of state, or states themselves brought down to decay, ruin has taught me thus to reflect, that time will take my love away also. This thought is as a death to me, since it cannot choose but lament to have that which it knows it must lose.

This particular group of sonnets about the ravages of time reaches its climax with this fine — and famous — one. It has historical as well as psychological interest. We can tell, from the frequent references in his works, that Shakespeare was interested by the monuments, the castles, churches, tombs, he saw as he went about the country. This, the latter half of the sixteenth century, was a sad time—like today—for a sensitive person to be travelling about England, observing the ravages wrought upon the monuments of the past. This sonnet draws our attention to the abbey-towers thrown down by the Reformation, the splendid brasses ripped out of the churches by the fury of the Reformers and the avarice of others.

The theme of land and water gaining upon each other Shakespeare derived from Golding's Ovid, which he was reading at this time for *Venus and Adonis* — it is the poem's source. Compare ll. 5-10 with Golding, *Metamorphoses*, XV. 288-90 :

> Even so have places oftentimes
> exchangèd their estate,
> For I have seen it sea which was
> substantial ground alate :
> Again where sea was, I have seen
> the same become dry land.

65

Since brass, nor stone, nor earth, nor boundless sea,
But sad mortality o'er-sways their power,
How with this rage shall beauty hold a plea
Whose action is no stronger than a flower?
O, how shall summer's honey breath hold out
Against the wreckful siege of battering days,
When rocks impregnable are not so stout,
Nor gates of steel so strong, but Time decays?
O fearful meditation! where, alack,
Shall Time's best jewel from Time's chest lie hid?
Or what strong hand can hold his swift foot back?
Or who his spoil of beauty can forbid?
    O, none, unless this miracle have might,
    That in black ink my love may still shine bright.

65

Since brass and stone, earth and boundless sea, are subject to mortality, how can beauty withstand that force, when its strength is no greater than a flower's? Or how shall the honeyed breath of summer hold out against the battering storm of time, when rocks and gates of steel are not so strong but time decays them. A fearful thought! for where, alas, shall Time's best jewel be hid from Time's chest? Or what strong hand can stay his swift foot? Or who can arrest his ravages upon beauty? None, unless there is hope in this miracle, that my love may ever shine bright out of this black ink.

An antiphon to the previous, more powerful, sonnet. It needs no comment, but we may point out how conscious Shakespeare is of the image of a jewel in a chest, cf. Sonnets 48 and 52 ; it appears in 2 *Henry VI*, III. ii. 409-10 :

> A jewel, locked into the woefull'st cask
> That ever did contain a thing of worth ;

as also in *Richard II*, and *King John*.

66

Tired with all these, for restful death I cry,
As, to behold desert a beggar born,
And needy nothing trimmed in jollity,
And purest faith unhappily forsworn,
And gilded honour shamefully misplaced,
And maiden virtue rudely strumpeted,
And right perfection wrongfully disgraced,
And strength by limping sway disabled,
And art made tongue-tied by authority,
And folly, doctor-like, controlling skill,
And simple truth miscalled simplicity,
And captive good attending captain ill :
    Tired with all these, from these would I be gone,
    Save that to die, I leave my love alone.

66

Weary with thinking of these things, I am ready to give up: to see merit born poor, for example, and the unworthy flourishing in jollity; to see faith betrayed and bright honour put down, innocent virtue abused, perfection wrongfully demeaned; to see strength crippled by limping power, art tongue-tied by authority, and pretentious stupidity in control of intelligence; to see simple truth regarded as simpleness of mind, and good dancing attendance upon evil in command. Weary with all this, I would willingly be gone, except that in dying I should leave my love alone.

———

Here Shakespeare provides his patron with something new. This curious sonnet shows the poet speaking out in his own person, Shakespeare as an Angry Man. We mark his resentment at merit being born poor, and nullity flourishing. There is a personal tone in all this, particularly the writer resenting 'art made tongue-tied by authority, and folly, doctor-like, controlling skill'. It has been thought that this was a reference to the censorship of the stage; but it is more likely to be a generic reference to the restrictions of authority upon art and thought in all times and places, for 'art' with Shakespeare means generally the arts and sciences, letters and learning, as well as technique. At any rate, he is speaking out what he really feels in the discouraging circumstances of 1592-3, in a mood of depression and resentment. At the end, he contrives a compliment to his young patron.

L. 12 echoes Marlowe's

And all his captains bound in captive chains,

Tamburlaine, Part I, III. iii. 115.

67

Ah, wherefore with infection should he live
And with his presence grace impiety,
That sin by him advantage should achieve
And lace itself with his society ?
Why should false painting imitate his cheek,
And steal dead seeing of his living hue ?
Why should poor beauty indirectly seek
Roses of shadow, since his rose is true ?
Why should he live, now nature bankrupt is,
Beggared of blood to blush through lively veins ?
For she hath no exchequer now but his,
And, proud of many, lives upon his gains.
    O, him she stores, to show what wealth she had
    In days long since, before these last so bad.

67

Why should he live with these infections of the time, and grace its ills with his presence, that sin may derive advantage from him and embellish itself with his society ? Why should false painting imitate his complexion and steal a lifeless appearance from his living colour ? Why should poor beauty imitate painted roses, when his rose is natural ? Why should he live now that nature is bankrupt and beggared of blood to course through living veins ? For she has no resources now but his and, in spite of her pride, lives upon him. She stores him up, to show what wealth she once had, before these evil days.

This somewhat far-fetched sonnet continues the thought of the preceding one and develops its reflections upon the age. Shakespeare, like Spenser, disapproved of the new fashion of painting in women. It is consoling for us to find Shakespeare out of patience with his time too.

68

Thus is his cheek the map of days outworn,
When beauty lived and died as flowers do now,
Before these bastard signs of fair were born,
Or durst inhabit on a living brow :
Before the golden tresses of the dead,
The right of sepulchres, were shorn away
To live a second life on second head,
Ere beauty's dead fleece made another gay :
In him those holy antique hours are seen,
Without all ornament, itself and true,
Making no summer of another's green,
Robbing no old to dress his beauty new ;
    And him as for a map doth nature store,
    To show false art what beauty was of yore.

68

And so his countenance is a pattern out of the olden time, when beauty lived and died as flowers do nowadays, before false hair was worn or dared decorate a living brow : before the tresses of the dead, the prerogative of tombs, were shorn to live again on others' heads, in days before beauty's locks made another gay. In him that ancient time is seen, without any ornament, true to itself, not decking out its summer with another's green, or robbing the old to dress up new beauty. So nature uses him as a map, to show false art what beauty was of old.

This subject, the shearing of locks from the dead to provide false hair for the living, gives the ingenious poet matter for another couple of sonnets for his patron. Very appropriately for Southampton, whose own golden tresses were a marked, but natural, feature. The theme is reflected not long after in *The Merchant of Venice*, III. ii. 92-6 :

> So are those crispèd, snaky, golden locks . . .
> Upon supposèd fairness, often known
> To be the dowry of a second head,
> The skull that bred them in the sepulchre.

L. I has a couple of reflections in *Lucrece*, l. 1712 :

> The face, that map which deep impression bears ;

and l. 1350,

> this pattern of the worn-out age.

69

Those parts of thee that the world's eye doth view
Want nothing that the thought of hearts can mend ;
All tongues, the voice of souls, give thee that due,
Uttering bare truth, even so as foes commend.
Thy outward thus with outward praise is crowned ;
But those same tongues that give thee so thine own
In other accents do this praise confound,
By seeing farther than the eye hath shown.
They look into the beauty of thy mind
And that, in guess, they measure by thy deeds ;
Then churls, their thoughts, although their eyes were kind,
To thy fair flower add the rank smell of weeds ;
   But why thy odour matcheth not thy show,
   The soil is this : that thou dost common grow.

69

Those parts of you that the world can see leave nothing that people's thought can improve on : all voices give you that due — it is but the truth that even enemies cannot deny. Thus the outer man is yielded outward praise. But those same voices mingle with it quite another accent when they look further than the eye sees. They look into your mind, measuring it in imagination by your deeds; and so their churlish thoughts, although outwardly friendly, add the rank smell of weeds to your fair flower. But why the odour you give does not match your show, the ground is this: you make yourself common.

————

Here is a bit of straight talk of a tutorial kind from an older man to a younger, however grand. Shakespeare gives him a piece of his mind, even if wrapped up in compliments : it says much for the poet's essential independence of spirit.

70

That thou art blamed shall not be thy defect,
For slander's mark was ever yet the fair ;
The ornament of beauty is suspect,
A crow that flies in heaven's sweetest air.
So thou be good, slander doth but approve
Thy worth the greater, being wooed of time ;
For canker-vice the sweetest buds doth love,
And thou present'st a pure unstainèd prime.
Thou hast passed by the ambush of young days
Either not assailed, or victor being charged :
Yet this thy praise cannot be so thy praise,
To tie up envy evermore enlarged.
   If some suspect of ill masked not thy show,
    Then thou alone kingdoms of hearts shouldst owe.

70

That you are blamed is not in itself a defect, for the fair were ever the target of slander; suspicion goes regularly along with beauty, a crow winging its way in the pure air. So long as you are good, slander only proves your worth the greater, since the time is so inviting; for vice, like canker, likes the sweetest buds, and you offer an unstained prime. You have passed by the ambush of your earliest youth either not tempted or, if so, not having fallen : yet this just praise cannot stop envy that is always on the alert. If some blemish did not touch your appearance, then you alone would possess whole kingdoms of hearts.

———

That these sonnets are in sequence is obvious. We see again the rhythm of reproach followed by forgiveness, natural to Shakespeare : he cannot blame the young man too much. Yet we cannot but observe that reflections are beginning to be made on Southampton ; and we remember that some eighteen months later, in June 1594, that sage young lady, Lady Bridget Manners, would not consider either Southampton or the Earl of Bedford as a mate — 'they be so young, and fantastical, and would be so carried away . . . she doubteth their carriage of themselves' (*Hist. MSS. Com.*, *Rutland*, I. 321). On Shakespeare's side we note his concern for Southampton's good. Marlowe's *Hero and Leander*, ll. 285 foll., offers a comparison with l. 2 :

> Whose name is it . . .
> So she be fair, but some vile tongues will blot ?

71

No longer mourn for me when I am dead
Than you shall hear the surly sullen bell
Give warning to the world that I am fled
From this vile world with vilest worms to dwell :
Nay, if you read this line, remember not
The hand that writ it ; for I love you so
That I in your sweet thoughts would be forgot
If thinking on me then should make you woe.
O if, I say, you look upon this verse
When I perhaps compounded am with clay,
Do not so much as my poor name rehearse,
But let your love even with my life decay :
   Lest the wise world should look into your moan,
   And mock you with me after I am gone.

When I am dead, do not mourn for me longer than you shall hear
the sullen bell give warning that I am gone from the world to dwell
with the worms. If you read this line, do not even remember the
hand that wrote it ; for I love you so that, if thinking of me made
you grieve, I would rather be forgotten from your thoughts. If you
should look upon these verses, when I perhaps am blended with
clay, do not even recall my name, but let your love decay with my
life ; lest the wise world should pry into your grief, and mock you
with my name after I am gone..

———————

This famous poem begins a sequence in which Shakespeare turns to con-
sider himself, the older man, in the relationship. As always with poets, it
moves him to finer poetry. It is perhaps natural, in the circumstances into
which the relationship has moved, that Shakespeare should write in this
mood of departure and of his own death. This elegiac mood about them-
selves has always moved poets to their best efforts — Milton's 'Lycidas',
Shelley's 'Adonais', Arnold's 'Thyrsis', are even more elegies for them-
selves, or their lost youth, than for their dead friends. This moving sonnet
has had its influence in subsequent literature : one hears it in the sonnets
of Christina Rossetti as in the virtual sonnet-forms of Tennyson's *In
Memoriam*. But, with Shakespeare, there is always the actor–dramatist's
self-awareness, half playing a part, suggesting another dimension, a mirror-
world.

72

O, lest the world should task you to recite
What merit lived in me that you should love
After my death, dear love, forget me quite,
For you in me can nothing worthy prove.
Unless you would devise some virtuous lie,
To do more for me than mine own desert,
And hang more praise upon deceasèd I
Than niggard truth would willingly impart.
O, lest your true love may seem false in this,
That you for love speak well of me untrue,
My name be buried where my body is,
And live no more to shame nor me nor you.
  For I am shamed by that which I bring forth,
  And so should you, to love things nothing worth.

72

Lest the world should put you to some effort to explain what merit there was in me that you should love on after my death, dear love, forget me, for you can prove nothing worthy in me. Unless you would invent some virtuous lie to do more for me than I deserve, and devolve more praise upon me than the scant truth allows. Lest your love seem false in speaking well of me untruly, let my name be buried with my body and live no more to shame either me or you. For I am ashamed of the figure I make — as you should be, to love what is worth nothing.

———

This sonnet is the echo of the preceding one, and develops the theme of what the world thinks. Where Sonnet 71 is inspired, is *donné* — in Valéry's phrase — Sonnet 72 is made. Nevertheless, it has feeling, as well as mastery. Notice the conciseness and the authority, in l. 1, of the phrase, 'should task you', and in l. 13 we are given a glimpse of Shakespeare's deprecation of his own conduct, a theme which will be developed later. Though there is something of inverted commas in Shakespeare's self-deprecation, his writing himself down, as against his expressed confidence in his verse, there is sincerity also. It is this ambivalence, the unconscious sincerity in a completely conscious, self-aware context, that makes the Sonnets of Shakespeare so difficult for ordinary folk to grasp.

73

That time of year thou mayst in me behold
When yellow leaves, or none, or few, do hang
Upon those boughs which shake against the cold,
Bare, ruined choirs, where late the sweet birds sang.
In me thou see'st the twilight of such day
As after sunset fadeth in the west,
Which by and by black night doth take away,
Death's second self, that seals up all in rest.
In me thou see'st the glowing of such fire
That on the ashes of his youth doth lie
As the death-bed whereon it must expire,
Consumed with that which it was nourished by.
    This thou perceiv'st, which makes thy love more strong
    To love that well which thou must leave ere long.

73

In me you behold that time of year when a few yellow leaves or none or few hang on the branches, shaking in the cold, like bare, ruined choirs, where lately birds were singing. In me you see such twilight as there is after the sun has faded in the west, which by and by is extinguished by night — image of death, that seals up all. In me you see the glow of embers, the ashes of my youth, dying out as on a death-bed, consumed by that which nourished it. Seeing this increases your love and makes you value more that which you must take leave of before long.

———

This familiar and much admired sonnet offers no difficulties. 'Bare, ruined choirs' brings to the eye the roofless shells of monastic churches which stood out rawly to anyone travelling round England in the latter part of the sixteenth century ; and 'where late the sweet birds sang' carries a characteristic double suggestion of the vanished singing. This seems to be a winter sonnet, the winter of 1592-3.

74

But be contented : when that fell arrest
Without all bail shall carry me away,
My life hath in this line some interest,
Which for memorial still with thee shall stay.
When thou reviewest this, thou dost review
The very part was consecrate to thee :
The earth can have but earth, which is his due,
My spirit is thine, the better part of me :
So then thou hast but lost the dregs of life,
The prey of worms, my body being dead,
The coward conquest of a wretch's knife,
Too base of thee to be rememberèd.
    The worth of that is that which it contains,
    And that is this, and this with thee remains.

74

Be contented : when the fatal summons of death, without any appeal, carries me away, my life has some share in these lines which will remain with you for a memorial. When you look them over, you see the very part that was consecrated to you : the earth can have but earth, its due ; the spirit is yours, the better part of me. So then you will have lost but the dregs of life, the prey of worms, my body being dead, the poor victim of time, too base to be remembered by you. The worth is in what it contains, and that is my verse, which remains with you.

This is a kind of *envoi* to the preceding group, in which Shakespeare is reflecting on himself and death. What can have put this so much in mind at this moment ? It provided a theme, of course ; but also it is the natural outcome of a mood of depression, in the winter of 1592–3. We notice again the constant contrast between the modest view of himself as a man and the confidence in himself as a poet. How well justified when one thinks of the immense variety of the Sonnets, the number and facility of the variations on their theme ! No doubt Southampton was providing something in return for them.

75

So are you to my thoughts as food to life,
Or as sweet-seasoned showers are to the ground ;
And for the peace of you I hold such strife
As 'twixt a miser and his wealth is found :
Now proud as an enjoyer, and anon
Doubting the filching age will steal his treasure ;
Now counting best to be with you alone,
Then bettered that the world may see my pleasure ;
Sometime all full with feasting on your sight,
And by and by clean starvèd for a look :
Possessing or pursuing no delight,
Save what is had or must from you be took.
    Thus do I pine and surfeit day by day,
      Or gluttoning on all, or all away.

75

You are to my thoughts as food to life, or as summer showers to the ground ; and for your sake I experience the conflict between a miser and his wealth : now proud to possess it, and then fearing the thieving age will steal his treasure ; now counting it best to have you alone to myself, then proud that the world sees my delight ; sometimes full with feasting on your sight, and next clean starved for a look; possessing no pleasure and pursuing none save what is had from you. And so alternately I starve and surfeit, having either everything, or else nothing at all.

This little-quoted sonnet tells us a good deal. In the first place there is the gratitude of a writer — to whom everything is food for the imagination, even pain and grief — for inspiration and for a subject. Then there is the alternating pleasure and disquietude in the relationship, with perhaps the first hint that Southampton may be taken away from Shakespeare by the competition of others. 'The filching age' describes the situation aptly, for there was keen competition for a patron, when it was sometimes a question of survival for a poet. This sonnet inaugurates a new sequence, in which the literary situation becomes the dominating theme : the appearance of a rival poet on the scene, who threatens to take Shakespeare's place in his patron's favour.

76

Why is my verse so barren of new pride,
So far from variation or quick change ?
Why with the time do I not glance aside
To new-found methods and to compounds strange ?
Why write I still all one, ever the same,
And keep invention in a noted weed,
That every word doth almost tell my name,
Showing their birth and where they did proceed ?
O, know, sweet love, I always write of you,
And you and love are still my argument :
So all my best is dressing old words new,
Spending again what is already spent :
   For as the sun is daily new and old,
   So is my love still telling what is told.

76

Why is my verse devoid of new invention, without variation or change ? Why do I not follow the fashion and try new techniques and far-fetched words ? Why do I always write in the same manner, and keep to an easily recognisable style, so that every word almost tells my name and where it came from ? The reason is that I always write of you, and you and love are ever my theme : so that my best endeavour is but dressing up old words anew, spending again what has already been spent. For as the sun is both new and old every day, so my love tells over what is already told.

Still more informative. We see that Shakespeare held to a more traditional course in the 'quick change' of verse-techniques developing in the 1590s, and thought of himself as a conservative, not one of the innovators, in the poetry of the period. We also see that by this time his own style was easily recognisable as his and 'doth almost tell my name'. His name by now was well known for his plays — witness Robert Greene's attack on him ; he had already written the three parts of *Henry VI*, *The Comedy of Errors*, *The Two Gentlemen of Verona*, *Titus Andronicus*, and *The Taming of the Shrew*. But, from Southampton's point of view, he might be wanting a change by now — and in this lay some uncertainty for his poet.

77

Thy glass will show thee how thy beauties wear,
Thy dial how thy precious minutes waste ;
The vacant leaves thy mind's imprint will bear,
And of this book this learning mayst thou taste :
The wrinkles which thy glass will truly show
Of mouthèd graves will give thee memory ;
Thou by thy dial's shady stealth mayst know
Time's thievish progress to eternity.
Look, what thy memory cannot contain
Commit to these waste blanks, and thou shalt find
Those children nursed, delivered from thy brain,
To take a new acquaintance of thy mind.
    These offices, so oft as thou wilt look,
    Shall profit thee and much enrich thy book.

77

Your glass will show you how your looks wear, your pocket dial how your time goes by ; the vacant leaves of this book you may fill up, while from it you may learn this : the wrinkles shown in your glass will bring to mind open graves ; by the shadow of your dial stealing onward you may know time's thievish progress to eternity. Commit what your memory cannot contain to these blank pages, and you will find your thoughts — those children of your brain — making a new impression on your mind. To consult glass and dial will profit you : the thoughts that arise will much enrich your book.

What an interesting sonnet, for all the conventionality of the thought. For it shows us Shakespeare presenting Southampton with a blank book in which to note down his thoughts, encouraging him to write — a very tutorial frame of mind, and perhaps more characteristic of the relationship than has been realised. It inaugurates a new sequence dominated by the competition of other poets, one in particular, for Southampton's favour.

78

So oft have I invoked thee for my muse,
And found such fair assistance in my verse,
As every alien pen hath got my use
And under thee their poesy disperse.
Thine eyes, that taught the dumb on high to sing
And heavy ignorance aloft to fly,
Have added feathers to the learned's wing
And given grace a double majesty.
Yet be most proud of that which I compile,
Whose influence is thine and born of thee :
In other works thou dost but mend the style,
And arts with thy sweet graces gracèd be.
    But thou art all my art, and dost advance
    As high as learning my rude ignorance.

78

I have invoked you so often as my theme and found such inspiration
for my verse that other pens have taken up my habit and broadcast
their poetry under your protection. Your eyes, that taught dumb
and ignorant me to sing, have inspired the learned and given double
power to their grace. Yet be proudest of what I compose, for it is
wholly born of you : in other works you serve but to improve the
style, their art is graced with the graces you lend them. But you are
all my art, and make my ignorance equal to learning.

———

This again takes us into Shakespeare's inner feeling about himself and his
work. Ll. 3-4 corroborate Francis Meres' well-known reference some
years later, in 1598, to the circulation of Shakespeare's 'sugared sonnets
among his private friends'. He himself implies that it was this that en-
couraged other poets too to hope for Southampton's patronage. But the
sonnet is most interesting for its confirmation of Shakespeare's consistent
attitude of resentment at his own retarded beginnings, the circumstances
that had made him no university wit — unlike Marlowe, Greene,
Nashe, Peele, Lyly, Lodge, and so many others. He had had to make his
way himself, without a university education — the significance of the
reference to 'the learned'. It was literally true, ll. 13-14, that it was
Southampton's friendship and the *entrée* to Southampton House that
made all the difference. But now Shakespeare's position as Southamp-
ton's acknowledged poet is under challenge, and for him a new situation
develops.

79

Whilst I alone did call upon thy aid
My verse alone had all thy gentle grace ;
But now my gracious numbers are decayed
And my sick muse doth give another place.
I grant, sweet love, thy lovely argument
Deserves the travail of a worthier pen ;
Yet what of thee thy poet doth invent
He robs thee of, and pays it thee again.
He lends thee virtue, and he stole that word
From thy behaviour ; beauty doth he give,
And found it in thy cheek ; he can afford
No praise to thee but what in thee doth live.
    Then thank him not for that which he doth say,
    Since what he owes thee thou thyself dost pay.

79

While I alone called upon your aid, my verse was alone in possessing all your grace; but now it is losing that quality, and my stricken muse is giving place to another. I grant, my dearest, that the theme of you is worthy of a better pen; yet what your poet invents he takes from you: he is but paying it back. He lends you virtue—a word he stole from your behaviour; he gives you beauty—and found it in your countenance; he can give you no praise but what lives in you. Then you need not thank him for what he says, for what he owes you you yourself pay.

———

Here is the rival poet, anxious for Southampton's favour, and in a fair way to achieve it — Shakespeare refers to him as 'thy poet'. Shakespeare is ready to suggest, generously, that this man may be 'a worthier pen'. Who can this be? But one must never forget, with the actor-poet, the 'inverted commas', the playing a conscious part — and Shakespeare's friendly nature. The rivalry may well have been friendly.

The sonnet follows convincingly upon Sonnet 78: no need to suggest displacement, as some have done. From the aesthetic point of view notice the inspired chime of ll. 1-2, with effective repetition and internal rhyme.

80

O, how I faint when I of you do write,
Knowing a better spirit doth use your name,
And in the praise thereof spends all his might,
To make me tongue-tied, speaking of your fame !
But since your worth, wide as the ocean is,
The humble as the proudest sail doth bear,
My saucy bark, inferior far to his,
On your broad main doth wilfully appear.
Your shallowest help will hold me up afloat,
Whilst he upon your soundless deep doth ride ;
Or, being wrecked, I am a worthless boat,
He of tall building and of goodly pride.
   Then if he thrive and I be cast away,
   The worst was this : my love was my decay.

80

How I am discouraged in writing of you, knowing that a better spirit now uses your name, and exerts all his power in praise of you—making me tongue-tied in speaking you up! But your worth is wide as the ocean, and carries the humble as well as the proudest sail: so my small boat, much inferior to his, boldly puts out on your broad sea. Your smallest aid will keep me afloat, while he rides secure in the soundless depths of your favour; though, if wrecked, I am lost, he erect and bearing up proudly. If he thrives then and I am cast away, the worst was just that my love was my fall.

———

This takes us further into the situation now developing. The rival poet was getting ahead in Southampton's favour, and Shakespeare becoming discouraged. For he readily admits the superiority of the 'better spirit', the greater genius of his rival, and the ascendancy he enjoys. Shakespeare's position is still insecure and dependent on Southampton. We perceive how critical such a situation was, now in 1593. But who could the rival be whose superiority of genius Shakespeare was so ready to recognise ; and not only of genius, but of position ? For 'tall building', l. 12, is the regular Elizabethan term for a big fine vessel, which would ride secure in deep water, where Shakespeare's 'saucy bark', l. 7, is a light craft, in shallow waters, easily succoured but easily wrecked. Though there is an element of literary exaggeration in the language, and Shakespeare was courteous and friendly by nature, we recognise that underneath the challenge was serious.

81

Or I shall live your epitaph to make,
Or you survive when I in earth am rotten ;
From hence your memory death cannot take,
Although in me each part will be forgotten.
Your name from hence immortal life shall have,
Though I, once gone, to all the world must die :
The earth can yield me but a common grave,
When you entombèd in men's eyes shall lie.
Your monument shall be my gentle verse,
Which eyes not yet created shall o'er-read ;
And tongues-to-be your being shall rehearse,
When all the breathers of this world are dead :
    You still shall live — such virtue hath my pen —
    Where breath most breathes, even in the mouths of
    men.

Either I shall live to write your epitaph, or you will survive when I am laid in earth ; death cannot take your memory away from this, although everything of me will be forgotten. From this your name shall gain immortal life, though once I am gone I shall be dead to all the world : for me there is but a common grave, while you will lie entombed in men's eyes. My verse shall be your monument, which eyes not yet created shall read over; and tongues-to-be shall recall your being, when all those now breathing are dead: my pen has such power that you shall live, where breath most breathes, even in men's mouths.

———

It is natural that such a situation should call forth Shakespeare's best, and summon up his confidence in his verse, whatever diffidence he may feel about himself. The challenge spoke to his emotions, so that an inspired poem is produced, starts easily and goes straightforward with one impulse, with no difficulty, to its end envisaged from the beginning : all with simple and entire conviction. The affinity between Samuel Daniel and Shakespeare is close, and in Daniel's *Musophilus*, ll. 956 foll., we find him developing the idea in ll. 10-11.

Note that the contract for the Southampton monument at Titchfield is of just this date, 1593. On the marble Southampton appears as a boy in armour, the big tomb being to his grandparents and parents, whose effigies lie on top.

82

I grant thou wert not married to my muse,
And therefore mayst without attaint o'er-look
The dedicated words which writers use
Of their fair subject, blessing every book.
Thou art as fair in knowledge as in hue,
Finding thy worth a limit past my praise ;
And therefore art enforced to seek anew
Some fresher stamp of the time-bettering days.
And do so, love ; yet when they have devised
What strainèd touches rhetoric can lend,
Thou, truly fair, wert truly sympathised
In true plain words by thy true-telling friend.
    And their gross painting might be better used
    Where cheeks need blood : in thee it is abused.

Notice the emphasis that is given, as before, to Southampton's fairness, and Shakespeare's honest truth. We may in turn emphasise again this characteristic of the Sonnets : they are more true, more real, more autobiographical, than any of the literary sonnet-sequences. The subtlety is that Shakespeare's have literary touches, but — so like him — they are life, not only literature. It is beside the mark to study them as a literary sonnet-sequence, sources and all that : properly a secondary approach.

From this we learn that the writers out for Southampton's favour were intellectuals. This is the meaning of the second quatrain, which implies also that Southampton wished to move with the fashion, and was flattered by their praise of his intellectual qualities. He was himself a university man, a Cambridge man. Shakespeare was an outsider. All this confirms the tradition that he was, in a sense, a 'child of nature' as against the intellectuals : which does not mean that he was uneducated, nor did it prevent him — a clever grammar-school boy, more teachable than they, and with more genius — from overtaking them. Notice, in the sestet, the emphasis he gives to his own essential truth as against the strained rhetoric of others, and that, in the last couplet he speaks out with real

82

I grant that you were not married to my muse and so may, without complaint, overlook the words which writers dedicate to their fair subject to bring a blessing upon their works. You are as fair in knowledge as in looks, in that achieving a value beyond my praise ; therefore are you forced to seek some newer tribute from these progressive days. You may do so, dearest ; yet, when they have thought up what strained touches rhetoric can lend, you, truly fair, were truly rendered in plain words by your true-telling friend. And their gross painting might be more in place where cheeks need blood : in you it is misused.

———

feeling and some indignation. 'And their gross painting might be better used' is a piece of plain speaking; nor can one fail to sense the edge in l. 8, 'Some fresher stamp of the time-bettering days'.

83

I never saw that you did painting need,
And therefore to your fair no painting set ;
I found, or thought I found, you did exceed
The barren tender of a poet's debt :
And therefore have I slept in your report,
That you yourself, being extant, well might show
How far a modern quill doth come too short,
Speaking of worth, what worth in you doth grow.
This silence for my sin you did impute,
Which shall be most my glory, being dumb ;
For I impair not beauty being mute,
When others would give life and bring a tomb.
    There lives more life in one of your fair eyes
    Than both your poets can in praise devise.

83

I never thought that you needed painting, and therefore added no painting to your fairness; I found, or thought I found, that you went beyond any offering a poet could make you in recompense. And therefore have I been negligent in your praise, that your existence in itself might show how far an ordinary pen falls short in celebrating your worth. You blamed me for this silence, which is most to my credit; for I do not impair beauty by keeping silent, when others would give life and their praise is as a tomb. There exists more life in one of your eyes than both your poets can invent.

———————

In these sonnets we see Shakespeare reviewing his work for Southampton in the light of the new situation, that of rivalry with another poet now also in favour : 'both your poets' clearly refers to Shakespeare and the other. In the next Shakespeare tells us that Southampton was 'fond on praise', and it seems that he meant to have both poets in train. For he has reproached Shakespeare with his silence — which the poet as usual turns into matter for a poem. Shakespeare's case for his own work is that it is natural and sincere, if plain, as against the rhetoric of his brilliant rival — and the implication is that he thought it insincere.

L7, 'modern' in Shakespearean English meant ordinary, or normal, every-day. Ll. 11–12 are quite outspoken.

84

Who is it that says most, which can say more
Than this rich praise, that you alone are you :
In whose confine immurèd is the store
Which should example where your equal grew ?
Lean penury within that pen doth dwell
That to his subject lends not some small glory ;
But he that writes of you, if he can tell
That you are you, so dignifies his story.
Let him but copy what in you is writ,
Not making worse what nature made so clear,
And such a counterpart shall fame his wit,
Making his style admirèd everywhere.
   You to your beauteous blessings add a curse,
    Being fond on praise, which makes your praises worse.

84

Who that says most can say any more than that you are yourself :
in whom is contained a store that can produce an example of
anything your equal ? It is a poor pen that does not lend some
small glory to its subject ; but he that writes of you that you are but
yourself gives dignity to his tale. Let him but copy what is written
in you, not making worse what nature made so clear, and such a
rendering shall win him fame for his wit and make his style every-
where admired. But to your blessings you add a curse, being fond
of praise, for that detracts from its value.

———

This duty-sonnet carries on the theme of the preceding ones, ingeniously
complimentary in their argument that Southampton needs no other praise
than that he is himself. The last couplet, which often clinches a sonnet
with something telling, emphasises the young peer's addiction to being
praised. The first quatrain gives considerable difficulty, and its punctua-
tion has been emended by all editors since Malone. I have merely
modernised on the basis of the original, without emendation, and given
the meaning that follows — following Shakespeare's intention.

85

My tongue-tied Muse in manners holds her still,
While comments of your praise, richly compiled,
Reserve their character with golden quill
And precious phrase by all the Muses filed.
I think good thoughts, whilst other write good words,
And like unlettered clerk still cry 'Amen'
To every hymn that able spirit affords
In polished form of well-refinèd pen.
Hearing you praised, I say ''Tis so, 'tis true',
And to the most of praise add something more ;
But that is in my thought, whose love to you,
Though words come hindmost, holds his rank before.
    Then others for the breath of words respect,
    Me for my dumb thoughts, speaking in effect.

85

My tongue-tied Muse keeps decently quiet while your praises are richly sung, upholding their quality in golden letters, in exquisite phrases polished by all the Muses. I think good thoughts, whilst another writes good words, and like an illiterate parish clerk I say 'Amen' to every poem that able spirit produces in admirable form from his accomplished pen. Hearing you praised, I say ' 'Tis so, 'tis true', and add something more to the height of your praise — but that is in my thoughts, where my love for you comes before words. Respect, then, others for the sound of their words, but me for my dumb thoughts speaking truthfully.

This is the last sonnet to deal with the rival poet in the present tense. We need not take with absolute literalness Shakespeare's description of himself as 'tongue-tied' before the genius of the other, for he continues to turn the situation to account in verse. Nevertheless, Shakespeare is having to take second place, echoing the praises of the other 'able spirit'. No doubt the young patron, avid of praise, welcomed something new and perhaps what else the newcomer had to offer. Shakespeare recognised his rival as a superior spirit: he is consistent in every reference to him in this. His claim for himself is only that he is superior in his love, in genuine devotion. L. 3 offers some difficulty: 'reserve their character' means preserve their characteristics; most editors have emended 'their' to 'your', but the original needs no emendation and I have kept to it. L. 9 has a parallel with *Venus and Adonis*, l. 851:

> She says ''tis so'; they answer all, ''tis so'.

86

Was it the proud full sail of his great verse,
Bound for the prize of all too precious you,
That did my ripe thoughts in my brain inhearse,
Making their tomb the womb wherein they grew?
Was it his spirit, by spirits taught to write
Above a mortal pitch, that struck me dead?
No, neither he, nor his compeers by night
Giving him aid, my verse astonishèd.
He, nor that affable familiar ghost
Which nightly gulls him with intelligence,
As victors of my silence cannot boast:
I was not sick of any fear from thence;
    But when your countenance filled up his line,
    Then lacked I matter: that enfeebled mine.

With this we reach a most important sonnet autobiographically
—the most difficult and the most rewarding: it enshrines a crisis in
Shakespeare's life and career. Any amount of commentary has been
devoted to it, mostly beside the mark. For observe that this sonnet is
written in the past tense: something has suddenly happened to the rival
poet; he is not mentioned again: he has disappeared; the rivalry is over.
We can only achieve certainty from a firm chronological foundation. We
have followed the Sonnets through 1592, through their references to
external events and their internal coherence with *Venus and Adonis* of
1592-3. We are now in 1593. There was only one contemporary whose
superiority was recognised; only one to whom the phrase, 'the proud
full sail of his great verse', could apply, confirmed by the strange particu-
lars of this sonnet. And, by the time of this sonnet, he is dead.

    Marlowe was killed in the tavern at Deptford on 30 May, and was
buried there on 1 June 1593. Shakespeare had that event in mind when he
wrote in *As You Like It*, III. iii. 12-13: 'It strikes a man more dead than a
great reckoning in a little room.'

86

Was it the proud full sail of his mighty verse, bound for the precious prize of much-loved you, that shut up my thoughts in my brain, leaving them there to germinate as in a tomb ? Was it his spirit, taught by spirits to write above a mortal pitch, that struck me dead ? No : neither he nor the spirits aiding him stunned my verse into silence. Neither he nor that friendly familiar that nightly gulls him with knowledge can boast that they beat me into silence : I was not discouraged by any fear from that quarter. But when your favour filled his verse, then I lacked inspiration : his enfeebled mine.

We learn from the second quatrain that the rival poet dabbled with the spirits. No one has ever satisfactorily explained ll. 9-10,

> that affable familiar ghost
> Which nightly gulls him with intelligence :

it refers to Mephistophilis, with his attendance on Dr. Faustus by night. Though Marlowe was dead, his play *Dr. Faustus* — in which Faustus is very much a projection of Marlowe — continued to be performed. Thus the present tense of 'nightly gulls him with intelligence' is in place in this sonnet in the past tense. The previous ll. 7-8 have hitherto resisted interpretation : 'his compeers by night giving him aid' is usually taken to refer to the corporeal night-companions of the rival poet. It is simply another way of expressing the idea in the previous ll. 5-6, 'by spirits taught to write above a mortal pitch'.

87

Farewell ! thou art too dear for my possessing,
And like enough thou know'st thy estimate :
The charter of thy worth gives thee releasing,
My bonds in thee are all determinate.
For how do I hold thee but by thy granting,
And for that riches where is my deserving ?
The cause of this fair gift in me is wanting,
And so my patent back again is swerving.
Thyself thou gav'st, thy own worth then not knowing,
Or me, to whom thou gav'st it, else mistaking ;
So thy great gift, upon misprision growing,
Comes home again, on better judgment making.
   Thus have I had thee, as a dream doth flatter,
   In sleep a king, but waking no such matter.

87

Farewell ! you are too dear for me to possess you, and likely enough
you know your own value : your very worth releases you, my claims
upon you are at an end.   For how can I hold you but by your own
grant, and how should I deserve that good fortune ? There is no
cause in me for such a gift, and so my privilege comes back to me.
You gave yourself, not then knowing your own worth, or else
mistaking me to whom you gave it.   And so your great gift, based
on a misunderstanding, comes home again, on better consideration.
So I have possessed you as in a flattering dream, thinking myself a
king, and waking up to find no such thing.

————

This sonnet reads like a conclusion to the previous section dominated by
the rivalry with Marlowe. In it Shakespeare seems to take a contingent
leave — though making a poem out of it, turning the material of the
experience to use. Ingenious as ever, here he plays variations on images
from the law — 'bonds . . . determinate', 'charter . . . releasing', 'patent',
'misprision', which means oversight or mistake, 'grant', and even 'gift'.

Observe the melancholy, farewell effect of all the feminine endings
of the line in present participles, no less than ten out of fourteen lines.
Psychologically, notice the double suggestion in the word 'dear' in l. 1,
meaning both too much beloved and too costly, and the piece of realism
without illusion of l. 2,

And like enough thou know'st thy estimate.

Light is thrown on the origin of the relationship by ll. 9-10 :

Thyself thou gav'st, thy own worth then not knowing,
Or me, to whom thou gav'st it, else mistaking.

Southampton as a youth had made a friend of the poet whom he had
taken on ; l. 10 has the interesting suggestion that he may have mistaken
his man : there was in Shakespeare an essential independence.

88

When thou shalt be disposed to set me light
And place my merit in the eye of scorn,
Upon thy side against myself I'll fight
And prove thee virtuous, though thou art forsworn.
With mine own weakness being best acquainted,
Upon thy part I can set down a story
Of faults concealed, wherein I am attainted,
That thou in losing me shalt win much glory :
And I by this will be a gainer too :
For bending all my loving thoughts on thee,
The injuries that to myself I do,
Doing thee vantage, double-vantage me.
　　Such is my love, to thee I so belong,
　　That for thy right myself will bear all wrong.

88

When you shall be disposed to regard me lightly and write down my worth to little value, I will contend on your side against myself and prove you upright, although faithless. Since I am best acquainted with my own weakness, on your behalf I can set down a tale of concealed faults, of which I am guilty, so that in losing me you shall be a gainer. And so shall I be too, for, directing all my thoughts on you, the injuries I do myself, in profiting you, will be of double profit to me. Such is my love, and so much do I belong to you, that to make you right I will bear all wrong.

———

After the strain between Shakespeare and his young patron over Marlowe, there is the implied reproach against Southampton's regarding him lightly, contingently exposing his worth to others' scorn — *i.e.* by letting him down. The implication that Southampton might be 'forsworn' is not a pleasant one, a stricture in spite of the protestations of love in which it is wrapped up.

89

Say that thou didst forsake me for some fault,
And I will comment upon that offence ;
Speak of my lameness, and I straight will halt,
Against thy reasons making no defence.
Thou canst not, love, disgrace me half so ill,
To set a form upon desirèd change,
As I'll myself disgrace ; knowing thy will,
I will acquaintance strangle and look strange ;
Be absent from thy walks ; and in my tongue
Thy sweet belovèd name no more shall dwell,
Lest I, too much profane, should do it wrong,
And haply of our old acquaintance tell.
   For thee, against myself I'll vow debate,
   For I must ne'er love him whom thou dost hate.

89

Say that you forsook me for some fault — and I will confess to the offence; say that I am lame, and immediately I will halt, putting up no defence against your charge. Dearest, you cannot disgrace me half so much, to give a pretext for a change you wish for, as I will disgrace myself. Knowing your will, I will deny acquaintance and appear a stranger; keep away from your walks; I will call no more upon your loved name, lest my common tongue should do it wrong and perhaps speak of our old acquaintance. I'll take up the debate against myself for you, since I must never love him whom you hate.

This carries forward Shakespeare's reflection upon the strain the relationship has undergone — with the references to the possibility of Southampton's parting with him, giving a pretext for a desired change.

    Phrases are reflected later in the plays. L. 6, 'to set a form', reappears in *King John*, V. vii. 26 ; l. 14 is virtually repeated in *Much Ado*, V. ii. 71, 'for I will never love that which my friend hates'. We are reminded of another aspect of the Sonnets — as a workshop for the plays, where complex personal relations and their expression were first worked out.

90

Then hate me when thou wilt ; if ever, now :
Now while the world is bent my deeds to cross,
Join with the spite of fortune, make me bow,
And do not drop in for an after-loss.
Ah, do not, when my heart hath 'scaped this sorrow,
Come in the rearward of a conquered woe ;
Give not a windy night a rainy morrow,
To linger out a purposed overthrow.
If thou wilt leave me, do not leave me last,
When other petty griefs have done their spite,
But in the onset come : so shall I taste
At first the very worst of fortune's might.
    And other strains of woe, which now seem woe,
    Compared with loss of thee will not seem so.

Then hate me when you will : if ever, now. Now, while the world is bent on crossing me, join in with the spite of fortune, and beat me down : do not come in with an after-blow. When my heart has recovered from one grief, do not come afterward with another, like a rainy day after a night of storm, to let me linger in disgrace already decided on. If you will leave me, do not leave me at the end, when other griefs have already worn me down ; but come at the outset — so that I shall feel the worst of my fate at the beginning. Then other causes for grief which now seem bad enough, compared with losing you, will not seem so.

———————

The relationship has become uneasy, never the same after the breach of trust over the mistress, still more over the rival poet. What is in question is whether Southampton will continue his favour and go on supporting his poet at this critical juncture, with the theatres continuing to be closed to the end of this year, 1593. This is the meaning of the reiterated emphasis on the 'spite of fortune', 'a purposed overthrow'. We have noted how much Shakespeare resented the ill-fortune of his beginnings ; now, when by 1592 he had achieved recognition and his plays were successful, the theatres were closed for most of these two plague years, 1592 and 1593, badly hitting him as both actor and dramatist dependent on them. How was he to live ? How was he living ? We have reason to suppose — to some extent on his patron's bounty. There can be no doubt about the seriousness of the matter — one hears its accents, anxiety, resentment, grief, in these Sonnets. In the midst of it all, one cannot but point out the naturalness of expression, the countryman's image, l. 7,

> Give not a windy night a rainy morrow —

so unlike Marlowe.

91

Some glory in their birth, some in their skill,
Some in their wealth, some in their bodies' force ;
Some in their garments, though new-fangled ill,
Some in their hawks and hounds, some in their horse.
And every humour hath his adjunct pleasure,
Wherein it finds a joy above the rest ;
But these particulars are not my measure :
All these I better in one general best.
Thy love is better than high birth to me,
Richer than wealth, prouder than garments' cost,
Of more delight than hawks or horses be ;
And, having thee, of all men's pride I boast :
    Wretched in this alone, that thou mayst take
    All this away and me most wretched make.

91

Some people take pride in their birth, some in their skill, some in wealth, some in strength of body ; some take pride in their clothes, fashionable though ill-becoming, some people in their hawks and hounds, others in their horses. Each temperament has its particular pleasure, which it enjoys above any other. But these individual tastes are not my line : I better them all in one best of all. To me your love is better than high birth, richer than wealth, prouder than the costliest clothes, of more delight than horses, hawks or hounds ; and having you, I boast of having more than all of them. I am wretched only in this, that you may take all this away and make me miserable.

———

This more relaxed little poem follows naturally enough on the heels of the previous, more urgent, one. Nevertheless, the apprehension remains and is given full expression in the concluding couplet, which is indeed the *clou* of the poem. It offers no difficulty, except in l. 3, 'new-fangled ill' : the Elizabethan phrase, new-fangled, which means new-fashioned, is still sometimes heard in country places. 'New-fangled ill' means fashionably unattractive. The phrase is consistent with Shakespeare's old-fashioned country tastes : we have already seen that he did not much care for new fashions, the taste for cosmetics, etc.

92

But do thy worst to steal thyself away,
For term of life thou art assurèd mine ;
And life no longer than thy love will stay,
For it depends upon that love of thine.
Then need I not to fear the worst of wrongs,
When in the least of them my life hath end ;
I see a better state to me belongs
Than that which on thy humour doth depend.
Thou canst not vex me with inconstant mind,
Since that my life on thy revolt doth lie :
O, what a happy title do I find,
Happy to have thy love, happy to die !
    But what's so blessèd-fair that fears no blot ?
    Thou mayst be false, and yet I know it not.

92

Do your worst to steal yourself away from me, yet you are mine for the term of my life ; my life will last no longer than your love, for it depends wholly upon it. So then I need not fear the worst of wrongs, when in the least of them I can make an end : a better state exists for me than that which depends on your humour. You cannot torment me with your inconstancy, since my life depends on your mood. O, what a right to be happy I have — happy to have your love, or else happy to die! But what is so fortunate that fears no mishap? You may be false, and I not know it.

———

What a revealing sonnet this is ! I do not think that its gravity, in the circumstances, has ever been grasped. It tells us quite clearly that Shakespeare's life will last no longer than Southampton's love, that it will come to an end with it. Things were as serious as that with Shakespeare in 1592–3. There was nothing remote in the idea of the death of a poet in those cruel years : indeed there was a high mortality among poets. In 1592 Thomas Watson and Robert Greene died ; in 1593 Marlowe, in the winter of 1593–4 Kyd, then Peele. What matter if one more were added to them ? There is the implication of the resigned tone of this sonnet, with Shakespeare accepting his fate either way. But what a shock it gives one to realise that he might have died in 1593, as well as Marlowe — and with all the work by which he lives unaccomplished ! There is reproach in ll. 8–9 — Shakespeare's understandable resentment at depending on a young man's humour, who had given evidence of his inconstancy in turning to Marlowe. In l. 10 the idea is carried on in the word 'revolt', which is cognate with revolution : the line means, literally 'since my life lies on your revolving round', or change of mind.

93

So shall I live, supposing thou art true,
Like a deceivèd husband ; so love's face
May still seem love to me, though altered new :
Thy looks with me, thy heart in other place.
For there can live no hatred in thine eye,
Therefore in that I cannot know thy change :
In many's looks the false heart's history
Is writ in moods and frowns and wrinkles strange.
But heaven in thy creation did decree
That in thy face sweet love should ever dwell ;
Whate'er thy thoughts, or thy heart's workings be,
Thy looks should nothing thence but sweetness tell.
   How like Eve's apple doth thy beauty grow,
   If thy sweet virtue answer not thy show !

93

So shall I continue like a deceived husband, supposing you to be true; so love's face may still seem love to me, though altered again: your looks with me, your heart elsewhere. For no hatred can exist in your eye, so that I cannot know your change by that: with many people the false heart betrays itself in their looks, in moods and frowns and unfriendly countenance. But heaven in creating you decreed that your face should express love; whatever your thoughts or your heart's workings may be, your looks speak nothing but sweetness. Your beauty would be a perfect Eve's apple if your goodness did not answer your appearance.

————

After an extremely serious sonnet, a lighter one : such is the rhythm. But the apprehension continues, and after the doubt, the fear of Southampton's turning away, things could hardly be the same. Still, what a tribute is paid to the young man's essential sweetness of nature in this sonnet : in the end his well-known generosity and loyalty came through and was fully borne out.

94

They that have power to hurt and will do none,
That do not do the thing they most do show,
Who, moving others, are themselves as stone,
Unmovèd, cold, and to temptation slow :
They rightly do inherit heaven's graces
And husband nature's riches from expense ;
They are the lords and owners of their faces,
Others but stewards of their excellence.
The summer's flower is to the summer sweet,
Though to itself it only live and die,
But if that flower with base infection meet,
The basest weed outbraves his dignity :
    For sweetest things turn sourest by their deeds,
    Lilies that fester smell far worse than weeds.

94

They that have power to hurt yet do not do it, that do not do what they give the appearance of doing, who attract others though they themselves are cold and unmoved, slow to temptation.: they rightly inherit heaven's graces, preserving nature's riches from waste ; they are the owners of themselves, where others are but caretakers of their endowments. The summer's flower is sweet, though it lives and dies only for itself; but if it becomes infected the coarsest weed surpasses it. For sweetest things turn sourest by what they do ; lilies that rot smell far worse than weeds.

———————

This powerful sonnet has a cutting edge to it. There is no reason to suppose that it is out of place, as has often been suggested : it continues the theme announced at the end of the previous sonnet — the doubt whether Southampton's virtue matched his outward appearance, and it links up with the next in which the doubt is confirmed, the reason made explicit. Is Shakespeare implying that Southampton is one of those

> Who, moving others, are themselves as stone?

Likely enough: he would not give himself to marriage; his flirtation with Shakespeare's mistress was a more superficial affair than the poet's passionate involvement ; later we know that he wished to get out of marrying Elizabeth Vernon. It is apparent that there was a good deal of narcissism in his make-up ; this is reflected in the theme and images of *Venus and Adonis* as throughout the Sonnets. Indeed it is the subject of the first section, 1-26.

L. 14 appears also in Peele's *Edward III*, II. i. 452 : an Elizabethan commonplace.

95

How sweet and lovely dost thou make the shame
Which, like a canker in the fragrant rose,
Doth spot the beauty of thy budding name !
O, in what sweets dost thou thy sins enclose !
That tongue that tells the story of thy days,
Making lascivious comments on thy sport,
Cannot dispraise but in a kind of praise :
Naming thy name blesses an ill report.
O, what a mansion have those vices got,
Which for their habitation chose out thee,
Where beauty's veil doth cover every blot
And all things turn to fair that eyes can see !
    Take heed, dear heart, of this large privilege :
    The hardest knife ill-used doth lose his edge.

95

How beguiling you make the shame, which, like blight in a rose, spots the perfection of your budding name. O, in what an envelope you enclose your sins ! The very tongue that reports how you spend your days, with malicious comments on your sport, cannot dispraise you but in a kind of praise : naming your name makes an ill report good. What a mansion those blemishes have which chose you for their habitation, where your looks cover every blot and give everything a fair appearance ! Take heed, dear heart, of this large liberty you have : the hardest knife loses it edge with ill use.

Here is the tutorial attitude towards the young man with a vengeance, nor need we have much doubt about the activities — the 'sins', l. 4, the 'vices', l. 9 — that disinclined him from marriage. L. 8 recalls the phrasing of Nashe's tribute to Spenser, in his *Strange News* of 1592 : 'his very name (as that of Ned Allen on the common stage) was able to make an ill matter good'. Shakespeare knew and read Nashe. Observe the internal rhymes in ll. 9-10, 'those' and 'chose', and the simple image of the last line.

96

Some say thy fault is youth, some wantonness,
Some say thy grace is youth and gentle sport ;
Both grace and faults are loved of more and less :
Thou mak'st faults graces that to thee resort.
As on the finger of a thronèd queen
The basest jewel will be well esteemed :
So are those errors that in thee are seen
To truths translated and for true things deemed.
How many lambs might the stern wolf betray,
If like a lamb he could his looks translate !
How many gazers mightst thou lead away,
If thou wouldst use the strength of all thy state !
    But do not so : I love thee in such sort
    As, thou being mine, mine is thy good report.

96

Some say that your fault is youth and some wantonness, others that youth and sport are graces in you; both grace and faults are loved alike by great and small: you make faults that appeal to you into graces. As the poorest jewel on the finger of a queen will be well thought of, so your errors are turned into qualities and taken as such. How many lambs might the wolf deceive if he could turn himself into the likeness of a lamb! How many admirers might you lead astray, if you were to use all the power of your rank and state! But do not do this: I love you so much that, as you are mine, mine is your good repute.

———————

The tutorial note continues, and how closely this is borne out by Lady Bridget Manners's objection to Southampton for a husband as 'so young and fantastical and would be so carried away' (cf. my *Shakespeare's Southampton*, 98.)

In ll. 5-6 Shakespeare had Queen Elizabeth in mind: one sees a flicker of the actor-dramatist performing before her, catching sight of a jewel. The concluding couplet is repeated from Sonnet 36: evidently the lines had so impressed themselves in his mind — an indication of how significant this way of thinking was to him in the relationship. Such a repetition, along with the misprints, corroborates that Shakespeare was not responsible for the eventual publication of the Sonnets.

97

How like a winter hath my absence been
From thee, the pleasure of the fleeting year !
What freezings have I felt, what dark days seen !
What old December's bareness everywhere !
And yet this time removed was summer's time,
The teeming autumn, big with rich increase,
Bearing the wanton burden of the prime,
Like widowed wombs after their lords' decease :
Yet this abundant issue seemed to me
But hope of orphans and unfathered fruit ;
For summer and his pleasures wait on thee
And, thou away, the very birds are mute ;
   Or, if they sing, 'tis with so dull a cheer
   That leaves look pale, dreading the winter's near.

How like winter has my absence from you been, the delight of the year now fleeting away ! How frozen I have felt, what dark days been through, the bareness of December around one everywhere ! And yet the previous time of absence was in summer and teeming autumn, heavy with fruitfulness, bearing the burden of the spring, like widows left with child by their lords. Yet all this fruitfulness seemed to me as if orphaned and unfathered : for summer and its pleasures wait on you and, with you away, the very birds are silent. Or, if they sing, it is with so little spirit that the leaves look pale, dreading the approach of winter.

———

This sonnet begins a new group, written in absence and, as it would appear, with the winter of 1593 ahead. In l. 5, 'this time removed' has an active sense, and would mean the previous time when Shakespeare was removed from being with or near Southampton : it seems then to refer to an absence during the summer and early autumn of 1592. Commentators have found difficulty with both the argument and the imagery. The argument is simple : absence from Southampton, whether in the approach of winter as now, or in summer and early autumn as before, makes Shakespeare sad. The different seasons have somewhat confused the imagery. L. 7 : 'the wanton burden of the prime' I have taken to refer to spring, when the fruits were wantonly, i.e. playfully, conceived ; but it might refer to harvest.

98

From you have I been absent in the spring,
When proud-pied April, dressed in all his trim,
Hath put a spirit of youth in every thing,
That heavy Saturn laughed and leaped with him.
Yet nor the lays of birds, nor the sweet smell
Of different flowers in odour and in hue,
Could make me any summer's story tell,
Or from their proud lap pluck them where they grew :
Nor did I wonder at the lily's white,
Nor praise the deep vermilion in the rose ;
They were but sweet, but figures of delight
Drawn after you, you pattern of all those.
   Yet seemed it winter still, and you away,
   As with your shadow I with these did play.

98

I have been absent from you in spring, when April, in all its coloured bravery, has put such a youthful spirit in everything that even heavy Saturn laughed and leaped. Yet neither the song of birds, nor the fragrance of flowers in their many colours, could make me tell a summer's tale, or pick the flowers from where they grew on the proud earth. Nor did I wonder at the white of the lily, nor praise the redness of the rose : they were but images of delight drawn after you, pattern of all of them. For it seemed winter still, with you away, as I played with these shadows of you.

It is not necessary to suppose, as some have done, that because this refers to a different absence in spring, the sonnet is misplaced. The point is that it continues the theme of absence, and though referring back to another separation in spring, is likely to have been written along with this group in the early winter of 1593. We have observed before how much and how often Shakespeare is away from Southampton : they would not have seen so much of each other as people suppose who do not know the circumstances of the age.

L. 7 refers to the intention of telling a summer's story, and thus to the germination of *A Midsummer Night's Dream*, which was produced for the marriage of the Countess of Southampton, 2 May 1594. L. 4 : the influence of Saturn was supposed to be gloomy and heavy — hence saturnine.

99

The forward violet thus did I chide :
Sweet thief, whence didst thou steal thy sweet that smells
If not from my love's breath ? The purple pride
Which on thy soft cheek for complexion dwells
In my love's veins thou hast too grossly dyed.
The lily I condemnèd for thy hand,
And buds of marjoram had stol'n thy hair ;
The roses fearfully on thorns did stand,
One blushing shame, another white despair ;
A third, nor red nor white, had stol'n of both,
And to his robbery had annexed thy breath ;
But, for his theft, in pride of all his growth
A vengeful canker ate him up to death.
    More flowers I noted, yet I none could see
    But sweet or colour it had stol'n from thee.

99

Thus did I chide the too early violet : Sweet thief, whence did you steal your fragrance, if not from my love's breath ? The purple of your complexion you have too grossly drawn from my love's veins. The lily I condemned compared with the whiteness of your hand, and buds of marjoram had stolen their colour from your hair ; the roses stood uneasily on thorns, one blushing shame, another white with despair ; a third, neither red nor white, had filched colour of both and added the fragrance of your breath ; but for his theft, in the pride of life a caterpillar ate him up in revenge. I noted still more flowers, but I could see none that had not stolen fragrance or colour from you.

This piece has a charming artificiality : it is an ingenious exercise in compliment, like the poems the poets of the early 1590s wrote to their ladies. But its literary interest is greater, for it is irregular — it has fifteen lines. It has been suggested that it is an unfinished draft, not properly reduced to shape. I do not think so ; for, notice, the first line is a prelude, an announcement ; then follows the sonnet. Ll. 5-6 are not easy, for they are elliptical and open to alternative interpretations. L. 7 would seem to indicate that Southampton's hair, a golden auburn in his portraits, curled naturally. There are parallels to l. 13 in both *Venus and Adonis*, 656, and *Romeo and Juliet*, II. iii. 30.

Where art thou, Muse, that thou forget'st so long
To speak of that which gives thee all thy might ?
Spend'st thou thy fury on some worthless song,
Dark'ning thy power to lend base subjects light ?
Return, forgetful Muse, and straight redeem
In gentle numbers time so idly spent ;
Sing to the ear that doth thy lays esteem
And gives thy pen both skill and argument.
Rise, resty Muse, my love's sweet face survey,
If Time have any wrinkle graven there ;
If any, be a satire to decay,
And make Time's spoils despisèd everywhere.
    Give my love fame faster than Time wastes life,
    So thou prevent'st his scythe, and crooked knife.

Some time has elapsed since Shakespeare wrote last.   Fairly certainly written — like all this group — in absence, the sonnet's theme is the effect of time, during this interval, upon the young patron.   Looking for the truth of fact under the proper form for complimentary verse in those days, we are struck by the truth of l. 2.   Many have noticed the marked contrast between Shakespeare's first, artificial, comedy, *The Comedy of Errors,* and the work that is connected with the Sonnets, *The Two Gentlemen of Verona, A Midsummer Night's Dream, Love's Labour's Lost, Romeo and Juliet*: a difference has been made by the intervening experience of life, the inspiration of love, with its accompanying exaltation and anguish, a dimension added to life.   We must also attend to the literal truth of ll. 7-8; Southampton appreciated Shakespeare's poetry.   And now there is no rival for favour, there is a relaxed tone in these sonnets: Shakespeare, like his Muse, is taking things more easily.   Moreover, in 1593, there was the marked success as a poet that he achieved with *Venus*

Where are you, my Muse, that you forget so long to speak of that which gives you all your power ? Do you waste your energy on some worthless theme, lowering your powers to light up some base subject ? Forgetful Muse, return and redeem in verse the time you have spent so idly ; sing to him who esteems your poetry, and gives your pen both skill and theme. Rise, slothful Muse, look into my love's countenance to see if Time has graven any furrow there ; if so, turn your satire against decay and make Time's ravages everywhere despised. Give my love fame faster than Time wastes life away, so that you forestall his scythe.

———

and Adonis. Ll. 3-4 give us Shakespeare's comment on what has been occupying him — writing plays, instead of poetry on a noble theme, *i.e.* to Southampton.

The easy, relaxed tone of these sonnets brings to mind the early tradition, coming through Davenant, that Southampton gave Shakespeare a handsome present 'to enable him to go through with a purchase which . . . he had a mind to' (cf. E. K. Chambers, vol. II. pp. 266-7). It is thought that it was this that enabled him to acquire a share in the Lord Chamberlain's company when it was formed in 1594, and this gave him financial security at last.

It would be expected for an Elizabethan patron to mark the dedications of *Venus and Adonis* and *Lucrece* with a gift; and that gives us, for our dating, precisely 1593 and 1594.

101

O truant Muse, what shall be thy amends
For thy neglect of truth in beauty dyed ?
Both truth and beauty on my love depends ;
So dost thou too, and therein dignified.
Make answer, Muse : wilt thou not haply say,
'Truth needs no colour, with his colour fixed ;
Beauty no pencil, beauty's truth to lay ;
But best is best, if never intermixed' ?
Because he needs no praise, wilt thou be dumb ?
Excuse not silence so, for't lies in thee
To make him much outlive a gilded tomb
And to be praised of ages yet to be.
   Then do thy office, Muse : I teach thee how
   To make him seem long hence as he shows now.

101

O truant Muse, what amends will you make for your neglect of truth-in-beauty? Both truth and beauty depend on my love; so do you too, and are the nobler for it. Make answer, Muse: will you not perhaps say, 'Truth needs no colouring, set down as it is with his colour; beauty needs no pencil, to lay on truth; each is best alone, without any mixture'? Because he needs no praise, will you be silent? Excuse it not thus, for it lies in you to make him out-live a gilded tomb and be praised by ages yet to come. Then do your duty, Muse: I teach you how to make him appear long hence as he appears now.

This continues the new turn Shakespeare gives to the theme, turning his silence, at any rate his writing less frequently, to account poetically. Naturally, after so many offerings, there is some repetition: ll. 10-12 repeat the argument of the famous Sonnet 55 and others. In ll. 1-2, notice the echo of 'truant' and 'truth'. So ingenious a master can permit himself the monosyllabic simplicity, the casual colloquialism, of the last line. Here is, perhaps, the 'gilded tomb' at Titchfield again in mind.

102

My love is strengthened though more weak in seeming,
I love not less, though less the show appear ;
That love is merchandized whose rich esteeming
The owner's tongue doth publish everywhere.
Our love was new, and then but in the spring,
When I was wont to greet it with my lays ;
As Philomel in summer's front doth sing,
And stops her pipe in growth of riper days :
Not that the summer is less pleasant now
Than when her mournful hymns did hush the night,
But that wild music burdens every bough,
And sweets grown common lose their dear delight.
    Therefore, like her, I sometimes hold my tongue,
    Because I would not dull you with my song.

My love is confirmed, though it appears less so ; in spite of appearances I do not love less : that love is cheapened whose value is everywhere extolled by the owner. Our love was new and but at the beginning when I used to greet it with my poems : as the nightingale sings in early summer, and ceases as the summer wears on. Not that the season is less pleasant now than when her mournful melody hushed the night, but that birdsong now burdens every bough, and delights grown common lose their appeal. Therefore, like her, I am sometimes silent, because I would not bore you with my verse.

———————

This turn of the theme is continued, in a relaxed, appeased mood. We learn something valuable : that the Sonnets began, it would seem from the imagery, in the spring, of 1592. We learn further, from l. 11, of the increase of this kind of poetry, of the sonnet vogue, in these years. The tone is retrospective, beginning to look back over the course of the friendship.

Ll. 3-4 have a parallel in *Love's Labour's Lost*, II. i. 15-16 :

> Beauty is bought by judgment of the eye,
> Not uttered by base sale of chapmen's tongues.

103

Alack, what poverty my Muse brings forth,
That having such a scope to show her pride
The argument, all bare, is of more worth
Than when it hath my added praise beside.
O, blame me not, if I no more can write !
Look in your glass and there appears a face
That over-goes my blunt invention quite,
Dulling my lines and doing me disgrace.
Were it not sinful then, striving to mend,
To mar the subject that before was well ?
For to no other pass my verses tend
Than of your graces and your gifts to tell.
    And more, much more, than in my verse can sit,
    Your own glass shows you when you look in it.

103

Alas, what a poor show my Muse puts up, that having such scope to prove her mettle, the subject in itself is worth more than when my praise is added to it. Do not blame me if I can write no more ! Look in your glass and you will see a face that goes quite beyond my blunt invention, making my lines dull and doing me discredit. Isn't it a mistake then, in striving to improve, to mar the subject that was very well before ? For my verses tend to no other end than to celebrate your gifts and graces. And when you look in your own glass it shows much more than there can be in my verse.

This shows Shakespeare conscious of coming to the end of his inspiration. After all, of this kind of verse there must some time come an end, and here he is repeating himself : we have had all that about the glass before, cf. Sonnet 77, for example. Even so, he turns his apology to account : matter for yet another offering, if not a very good one, to an expectant patron.

104

To me, fair friend, you never can be old,
For as you were when first your eye I eyed,
Such seems your beauty still : three winters cold
Have from the forests shook three summers' pride,
Three beauteous springs to yellow autumn turned
In process of the seasons have I seen,
Three April perfumes in three hot Junes burned,
Since first I saw you fresh, which yet are green.
Ah, yet doth beauty like a dial-hand
Steal from his figure, and no pace perceived ;
So your sweet hue, which methinks still doth stand,
Hath motion, and mine eye may be deceived :
    For fear of which, hear this, thou age unbred :
    Ere you were born was beauty's summer dead.

104

To me, my friend, you never can be old, for as you were when I first beheld you, such is your beauty still : three winters have shaken three summers' foliage from the forests, three springs have I seen turn to autumn in the procession of the seasons, three April perfumes burned up in three hot Junes, since first I saw you — and you are yet young. Still beauty moves on, like a dial-hand stealing forward and no movement seen ; so your looks, which seem to me unchanged, have motion, and my eye may be deceived. For fear of which, hear this, you age unborn : before ever you came into being beauty's summer was dead.

———

It is almost impossible to render this wonderful sonnet in any terms other than its own. Continuing this theme, the passage of time, Shakespeare finds inspiration in looking back nostalgically over the three years of the friendship to its beginning. So that gives us a date: we are now in the summer of 1594. The three winters of the friendship are those of 1591–2, 1592–3, 1593–4; the Aprils and Junes are those of 1592, 1593, 1594. Southampton was now twenty — he would be twenty-one and reach his majority in October 1594 — and was as beautiful as he had been at eighteen. But the dial-hand was moving on, as in Sonnet 77, and Shakespeare, now thirty, was repeating himself.

L. 4 is reflected in *Romeo and Juliet*, I. ii. 10;

> Let two more summers wither in their pride.

The image in l. 7, derived from burning perfumes in a house, reflects Shakespeare's increased sophistication with his acquaintance with high society and great houses.

105

Let not my love be called idolatry,
Nor my belovèd as an idol show,
Since all alike my songs and praises be
To one, of one, still such, and ever so.
Kind is my love today, tomorrow kind,
Still constant in a wondrous excellence ;
Therefore my verse to constancy confined,
One thing expressing, leaves out difference.
'Fair, kind, and true', is all my argument,
'Fair, kind, and true', varying to other words ;
And in this change is my invention spent,
Three themes in one, which wondrous scope affords.
   'Fair, kind, and true', have often lived alone,
   Which three till now never kept seat in one.

105

Let not my love be called idolatry, nor my beloved appear as an idol, because all my poems are written to one, of one, are still so and always will be. My love is kind today, as he will be tomorrow, ever constant in excellence ; therefore my verse is confined to constancy, expressing only one thing, leaving out all variation. 'Fair, kind, and true', is my whole theme, 'fair, kind, and true', sometimes in other words : my invention is spent in ringing these changes, three themes in one, affording infinite scope. 'Fair, kind, and true', have often existed separately, but never till now were all found in one.

———

This conventional enough sonnet still tells us something very important to know — that all Shakespeare's poems were written to and for Southampton, were about him and would continue to be so. This is, of course, a poet's exaggeration ; but it serves to bring home to us that Shakespeare, unlike Jonson and others, had only one patron, acknowledged in the dedications of his two poems, and no other.

106

When in the chronicle of wasted time
I see descriptions of the fairest wights,
And beauty making beautiful old rhyme
In praise of ladies dead and lovely knights,
Then in the blazon of sweet beauty's best,
Of hand, of foot, of lip, of eye, of brow,
I see their antique pen would have expressed
Even such a beauty as you master now.
So all their praises are but prophecies
Of this our time, all you prefiguring ;
And, for they looked but with divining eyes,
They had not still enough your worth to sing :
   For we, which now behold these present days,
   Have eyes to wonder, but lack tongues to praise.

106

When in chronicles of past time I see descriptions of the fairest persons, and old rhyme made beautiful by praise of dead ladies and handsome knights — then in beauty's best scutcheon, of hand and foot, of lip and eye and brow, I see their pens of old would have expressed just such a beauty as yours is now. So all their praises are but prophecies of this our time, prefiguring you ; and though they looked with eyes of divination, they still had not enough to sing your worth : while we in this present age have eyes to wonder, but lack the tongues to praise.

———

It is typical that commentators should not have noticed from this that Shakespeare was reading Chaucer, yet it is confirmed by the fact that he drew upon 'The Knight's Tale' for the plot of *A Midsummer Night's Dream* in this year 1593–4. Notice the consciousness of 'this our time' throughout the sestet, which carries forward to the famous sonnet following.

L. 12 : a number of editors have altered 'still' to 'skill' : there is no necessity. Though there is room for doubt, the change to 'skill' destroys the apposition, the contrasted sense, of the two last couplets.

107

Not mine own fears, nor the prophetic soul
Of the wide world dreaming on things to come,
Can yet the lease of my true love control,
Supposed as forfeit to a confined doom.
The mortal moon hath her eclipse endured,
And the sad augurs mock their own presage ;
Incertainties now crown themselves assured,
And peace proclaims olives of endless age.
Now with the drops of this most balmy time
My love looks fresh, and Death to me subscribes,
Since, spite of him, I'll live in this poor rhyme,
While he insults o'er dull and speechless tribes.
   And thou in this shalt find thy monument,
   When tyrants' crests and tombs of brass are spent.

Neither my own fears, nor the apprehensions of the world dwelling on what is to come, can yet determine the period of my love, supposed to be subject to mortality. The mortal moon has come through her eclipse, and the prophets of woe belie their own forecast ; uncertainties are now resolved, and the promise of permanent peace is proclaimed. Now with the dew of this balmy time my love looks fresh, and Death submits to me, since, in spite of him, I shall live in this verse, while he triumphs over dull, unlettered peoples. In this you shall find your monument when tyrants' crests and tombs of brass have crumbled away.

———

This sonnet rewards analysis, though all commentators have found its difficulties insurmountable. To the historian they are not ; their solution affords confirmatory evidence for the dating of the Sonnets. The convergence of the two historical events referred to in ll. 5-8 pinpoints the dating and makes it certain. To take ll. 7-8 first : these refer to the end of the long religious wars in France with the submission of Paris to Henri IV in March 1594 and the achievement of peace. In ll. 5-6 all Elizabethan scholars of any judgment recognise that 'the mortal moon' refers to Queen Elizabeth. She has come through an eclipse, a threat to her : as indeed she had this winter of 1593-4 with the Lopez conspiracy. Dr. Lopez, her personal physician, was found to be in touch with Spain with the idea of poisoning her, and he was executed in June 1594. These events made a great impression on Shakespeare's mind, as on other people's. The first contributed something to *Love's Labour's Lost* with the theme of Navarre's oath-breaking ; the second to *The Merchant of Venice* with its portrait of Shylock. We are then in the year 1594.

The amount of nonsense written about this famous sonnet, in the absence of precise dating, is ludicrous. Nor is there the slightest reason, let alone a compelling one, for removing it from its place in the sequence: it is in its proper place.

108

What's in the brain that ink may character
Which hath not figured to thee my true spirit ?
What's new to speak, what new to register,
That may express my love, or thy dear merit ?
Nothing, sweet boy ; but yet, like prayers divine,
I must each day say o'er the very same,
Counting no old thing old, thou mine, I thine,
Even as when first I hallowed thy fair name.
So that eternal love in love's fresh case
Weighs not the dust and injury of age,
Nor gives to necessary wrinkles place,
But makes antiquity for aye his page ;
    Finding the first conceit of love there bred,
    Where time and outward form would show it dead.

108

What's in the brain that may be written down in ink which has not described to you my true spirit ? What is there new to say that may express my love or your worth ? Nothing, dear friend ; but yet, like divine service, I must every day say over the same, counting nothing outdated, you mine, I yours, just as when first I blessed your name. So that love, being eternally new, takes no account of the dust and injury of age, nor gives place to inevitable wrinkles, but makes even old age its servitor ; finding the first impression of love still there, where time and outward appearance would suppose it dead.

Inspiration seems running short, and indeed what wonder ? Shakespeare admits as much in the octave, yet contrives to give the old theme a new turn in the sestet. Again he shows himself very self-conscious on the subject of 'wrinkles', several times mentioned already — perhaps understandably for an actor.

109

O, never say that I was false of heart,
Though absence seemed my flame to qualify :
As easy might I from myself depart
As from my soul, which in thy breast doth lie.
That is my home of love : if I have ranged,
Like him that travels, I return again ;
Just to the time, not with the time exchanged,
So that myself bring water for my stain.
Never believe, though in my nature reigned
All frailties that besiege all kinds of blood,
That it could so preposterously be stained
To leave for nothing all thy sum of good :
  For nothing this wide universe I call,
  Save thou, my rose ; in it thou art my all.

Do not say that I was false in heart, though absence seemed to make my love less warm — I might as easily depart from myself as from my soul, which lies in your breast. That is my love's home : if I have rangèd, like a traveller, I return home again : punctually to the time, not changing with the time, so that I myself bring water to wash away my stain. Though in my nature there reign all the frailties that besiege all kinds of blood, do not believe it could receive so preposterous a stain as to leave all your good for nothing : for I call the whole universe nothing without you, my rose ; in it you are all in all to me.

Very interesting autobiographically. It confirms that Shakespeare has been absent from Southampton, going about the country, and has been less attentive than of old in his offerings of duty. We detect a note of assured independence beneath the affection : with his share in the Lord Chamberlain's Company he now has security. In 1594 the theatres were active again, and it is clear from this and the next sonnet that Shakespeare was also on tour at some time this year. In these circumstances he may well have appeared to be neglectful ; but he returns from touring punctually to the time, l. 7. More interesting is the confession, ll. 9-10, of the frailties of his sportive blood, where he confirms the traditional stories and our knowledge of his ways with women. Nevertheless, he insists that his love is for Southampton alone, 'my rose'. No particular difficulties except perhaps for l. 7.

110

Alas, 'tis true I have gone here and there,
And made myself a motley to the view,
Gored mine own thoughts, sold cheap what is most dear,
Made old offences of affections new.
Most true it is that I have looked on truth
Askance and strangely ; but, by all above,
These blenches gave my heart another youth,
And worse essays proved thee my best of love.
Now all is done, have what shall have no end :
Mine appetite I never more will grind
On newer proof, to try an older friend,
A god in love, to whom I am confined.
   Then give me welcome, next my heaven the best,
   Even to thy pure and most most loving breast.

110

Alas, it is true that I have gone here and there and exposed myself as a jester on the stage, wounded my inmost feelings, sold cheap what is most dear, given offence to old affections by entertaining new ones. It is true that I have looked askance at truth ; but these digressions made me feel young again, and other experiences proved you my best love. Now all that is over, accept what shall be for good : I never more will whet my appetite on newer acquaintance, to try an older friend — a god in love to whom I am bound. Then give me a welcome, next heaven the best I know, even to your pure, loving heart.

Quite continuous and informative autobiographically : it shows us something of what Shakespeare had been up to while away on tour in the country in 1594, and what he felt about it. Once more he lets us into the secret of his feelings about his profession as an actor and confesses how much he minded making himself a motley to the view, exposing his own feelings, selling cheap what was most dear to him. In addition, he had been having other experiences in the realm of affection — which made him feel young again, but made him reproach himself in coming back to Southampton. L. 7 : the word 'blenches' means side-glances, a turning of the eye aside.

III

O, for my sake do you with Fortune chide,
The guilty goddess of my harmful deeds,
That did not better for my life provide
Than public means, which public manners breeds.
Thence comes it that my name receives a brand,
And almost thence my nature is subdued
To what it works in, like the dyer's hand :
Pity me then and wish I were renewed.
Whilst, like a willing patient, I will drink
Potions of eisel 'gainst my strong infection :
No bitterness that I will bitter think,
Nor double penance to correct correction.
    Pity me then, dear friend, and I assure ye
    Even that your pity is enough to cure me.

III

Chide Fortune for my sake — the goddess responsible for my ill deeds — that did not provide better for my life than a public profession, which breeds public manners. For with that is my name branded, and my nature almost subdued to what it works in, like the dyer's stained hand. Then pity me and wish I were made new again ; whilst, a willing patient, I will drink doses of vinegar against my strong infection. There is no medicine that I will think too bitter, nor refuse double penance to correct my failings. Pity me, dear friend, and I assure you that your pity even is enough to cure me.

———

This carries the theme of the previous sonnet a stage further and takes us into the recesses of the gentlemanly Shakespeare's resentment against having to follow the profession that brought him his fame. Even his name, he thinks, 'receives a brand' therefrom, his nature almost 'subdued to what it works in'. L. 10 refers to the use of vinegar as a prophylactic against the plague.

112

Your love and pity doth the impression fill
Which vulgar scandal stamped upon my brow ;
For what care I who calls me well or ill,
So you o'er-green my bad, my good allow ?
You are my all the world, and I must strive
To know my shames and praises from your tongue :
None else to me, nor I to none alive,
That my steeled sense or changes right or wrong.
In so profound abysm I throw all care
Of others' voices, that my adder's sense
To critic and to flatterer stoppèd are.
Mark how with my neglect I do dispense :
    You are so strongly in my purpose bred
    That all the world besides methinks are dead.

112

Your love and pity erase the mark which vulgar scandal stamped upon my brow ; for what do I care who calls me well or ill so long as you cover my bad and approve what is good ? You are all the world to me, and I must strive to know my faults and good points from your tongue : there is no one else to me, nor do I take anyone in the world into account, that changes my fixed determination, whether right or wrong. Into so deep an abyss I throw all care of others' voices, that like the adder I stop my ears to critic and flatterer alike. Mark how I excuse my neglect of you : you are so strongly entrenched in my mind that I consider all the world besides as dead.

———

This sonnet is no less interesting from the literary point of view. It refers back to Greene's attack upon Shakespeare in 1592 as an upstart actor taking the place of the playwrights and stealing their feathers. We know how keenly Shakespeare felt this from Chettle's apology for letting the reflections upon him appear in print : 'because myself have seen his demeanour no less civil than he excellent in the quality he professes. Besides, divers of worship have reported his uprightness of dealing, which argues his honesty, and his facetious grace in writing, that approves his art.' (q. Chambers, vol. II, p. 189.) No doubt Southampton had been one of the worshipful persons to vouch for his uprightness of dealing. The use of the word 'o'er-green', l. 4, Shakespeare's own coinage, makes it clear that this was 'the vulgar scandal' that had left its mark upon him. Still more interesting is Shakespeare's conclusion to pay no attention to 'others' voices', whether of critic or flatterer. How wise of him, especially to pay no attention to critics — or he might never have got his work done. It is nice to have here precisely what Shakespeare thought of them. Ll. 7-8 are difficult, for two sentences are telescoped together : I have extracted the sense.

113

Since I left you mine eye is in my mind,
And that which governs me to go about
Doth part his function and is partly blind,
Seems seeing, but effectually is out :
For it no form delivers to the heart
Of bird, of flower, or shape which it doth latch :
Of his quick object hath the mind no part,
Nor his own vision holds what it doth catch :
For if it see the rud'st or gentlest sight,
The most sweet favour or deformedest creature,
The mountain or the sea, the day or night,
The crow or dove, it shapes them to your feature.
 Incapable of more, replete with you,
 My most true mind thus maketh mine untrue.

113

Since I left you my eye is in my mind, and that which enables me to go about part performs its function and is part blind, seems to see but effectively is put out. For it presents to the mind no form of bird or flower, or shape that it grasps : the mind has no hold upon passing objects, nor does the vision retain what it perceives. Beholding the rudest or the gentlest sight, the most attractive or the most deformed appearance, mountain or sea, day or night, crow or dove, it shapes them to your likeness. Incapable of more, filled with the thought of you, the truest part of my mind makes me see things untruly.

————

Very much a duty-sonnet, rather artificial, written in absence ; we cannot but admire the ingenuity with which Shakespeare keeps the ball rolling. Beneath the protestations I think we can feel increasing independence from Southampton, an inevitable moving away in mind, however much his poet protests. The sonnet is not altogether easy, *e.g.* to catch the exact meaning of ll. 1-4. and l. 14. L. 1 has a parallel in *Lucrece*, l. 1426, 'save to the eye of mind'.

Or whether doth my mind, being crowned with you,
Drink up the monarch's plague, this flattery ?
Or whether shall I say mine eye saith true,
And that your love taught it this alchemy,
To make of monsters and things indigest
Such cherubins as your sweet self resemble,
Creating every bad a perfect best,
As fast as objects to his beams assemble ?
O, 'tis the first ; 'tis flattery in my seeing,
And my great mind most kingly drinks it up :
Mine eye well knows what with his gust is 'greeing,
And to his palate doth prepare the cup.
   If it be poisoned, 'tis the lesser sin
   That mine eye loves it and does first begin.

———

Rather far-fetched to our taste, and not really congenial to Shakespeare's.
Perhaps we see him not only struggling to say something new — difficult
enough in itself — but trying to respond to the increasingly metaphysical
strain among the younger poets, looking for more intellectual content in
verse than that which the early 1590s displayed. In l. 5, 'things indigest'
comes from a phrase of Ovid, that impressed itself upon Shakespeare's
mind from his schooldays : '*rudis indigestaque moles*', which appears in
3 Henry VI, where Gloucester is described as 'an indigested and deformed
lump'. More interesting is Shakespeare's pointed reference to flattery as
'the monarch's plague'. This cannot be without some thought of the
Queen in mind. Shakespeare's affiliation to Southampton brought him
into proximity with the opposition attitude towards her, and it was
observed at the time of her death that Shakespeare offered no tribute of
verse in her memory. She had kept Southampton in the Tower during
the last two years of her life, for his part in the Essex conspiracy. But

114

Perhaps my mind, being crowned with you, drinks up flattery — the plague of monarchs ? Or shall I say that my eye tells true and that your love taught it this alchemy, to turn monsters and mis-shapen things into such cherubins as resemble you, creating out of every ill object a perfect best, as fast as things pass before my sight ? It is the first, rather — flattery in my seeing, and like a monarch my mind drinks it up : my eye knows quite well what appeals to it, and prepares the cup according to taste : if it is poisoned, it is the lesser sin that my eye loves it and leads the mind on.

———

already during the period of the Sonnets she was expressing her disapproval of Southampton — for his virtual breach of promise to marry Burgh-ley's grand-daughter, for not taking up his family responsibilities, perhaps for his conduct in general. She must have known a thing or two.

Ll. 10-11 are fascinating psychologically. An early tradition tells us that Shakespeare played kingly parts. Once before, in Sonnet 87, we have seen him thinking of himself, in sleep, as a king. Who at this moment was flattering him ? I think it must refer to the very favourable reception of his two poems, each 'crowned with you', *i.e.* a dedication to Southampton.

115

Those lines that I before have writ do lie,
Even those that said I could not love you dearer ;
Yet then my judgment knew no reason why
My most full flame should afterwards burn clearer.
But reckoning Time, whose millioned accidents
Creep in 'twixt vows and change decrees of kings,
Tan sacred beauty, blunt the sharp'st intents,
Divert strong minds to the course of altering things :
Alas, why — fearing of Time's tyranny —
Might I not then say 'Now I love you best',
When I was certain o'er incertainty,
Crowning the present, doubting of the rest ?
   Love is a babe ; then might I not say so,
    To give full growth to that which still doth grow.

115

Those lines that I have written before lie — even those that said I could not love you dearer ; but then my judgment knew no reason why my full flame should burn more clearly afterwards. Only there was Time to take account of, whose innumerable accidents creep in between vows and change kings' decrees, darken beauty, blunt the keenest intentions, divert strong minds to different courses. Alas, fearing the tyranny of Time, why might I not say then, 'Now I love you best' — when after uncertainty I had achieved certainty, crowning the present, doubtful of everything else? Love is a child : might I not say so, to allow for full growth to what is still growing.

———

Also rather laboured ; and underneath the asseverations we cannot but feel that Shakespeare is moving away in mind. Still we learn something about the course of the relationship — that he had achieved certainty after a period of uncertainty. The crux of the somewhat strained argument is reached in the last couplet : why could I not, when I had achieved certainty, say 'Now I love you best ? ' Because love is as a child, whose full growth is to come, and my love still grows. At this point we may take leave to wonder.

116

Let me not to the marriage of true minds
Admit impediments : love is not love
Which alters when it alteration finds,
Or bends with the remover to remove.
O, no ! it is an ever-fixèd mark
That looks on tempests and is never shaken ;
It is the star to every wandering bark,
Whose worth's unknown, although his height be taken.
Love's not Time's fool, though rosy lips and cheeks
Within his bending sickle's compass come ;
Love alters not with his brief hours and weeks,
But bears it out even to the edge of doom :
 If this be error and upon me proved,
 I never writ, nor no man ever loved.

116

Let me not admit impediments to the marriage of true minds : love is not love which alters when it meets with alteration, or changes when one of them changes. No, it is a fixed beacon that looks on storms and is not shaken ; it is the star to every voyaging ship, whose value is not calculable although its altitude is. Love is not the sport of Time, though rosy lips and cheeks come within the compass of his sickle ; love does not alter with the days, but keeps straight on to the threshold of doomsday. If this be error proved against me, I never wrote and no man ever loved.

———

Shakespeare comes clear with this famous sonnet after the note of dubiety and apology in the previous ones. All the same, in spite of its confession of faith, or because of it, it sounds like a valediction. Ll. 1-2 reflect the marriage-service in the Prayer Book.

117

Accuse me thus — that I have scanted all
Wherein I should your great deserts repay,
Forgot upon your dearest love to call,
Whereto all bonds do tie me day by day ;
That I have frequent been with unknown minds,
And given to time your own dear-purchased right ;
That I have hoisted sail to all the winds
Which should transport me farthest from your sight.
Book both my wilfulness and errors down,
And on just proof surmise accumulate ;
Bring me within the level of your frown,
But shoot not at me in your wakened hate :
    Since my appeal says I did strive to prove
    The constancy and virtue of your love.

117

You may charge me with neglecting the duty I have to requite your
great deserts, forgetting to call upon your love, to which I am by
all bonds daily bound ; with frequenting strangers, and giving to
the world in general the right you purchased dearly ; with hoisting
sail to all the winds that take me farthest from you. Put down both
my wilfulness and my errors to my account, and add your suspicions
to what is justly proved against me ; bring me within the compass
of your disapproval, but do not shoot at me in your awakened
dislike : since my appeal is that I was striving to test the constancy
and trueness of your love.

This indicates something of a breach, and that Southampton had cause
for resenting Shakespeare's conduct. It is not difficult to read between
the lines that now that Shakespeare was secure, and in any case wholly
taken up with his work for the Lord Chamberlain's Company both as
actor and as playwright, he had not the time to give to his young patron
that he had had in the years 1592 and 1593. New prospects were opening
before him, new acquaintance which he would need to pursue and which
took him away from Southampton. The young patron clearly resented
this, since he had a 'dear-purchased right' to Shakespeare, on the score of
both love and financial support. L. 4, I think, may refer to the obligation
Shakespeare owed his patron for the purchase of a share in the Company,
since it is described as tying him 'day by day' ; but he confesses that 'all
bonds' tie him to his patron. L. 11 offers an interesting parallel with *A
Lover's Complaint*, ll. 309-10, where Southampton was in mind as the
attractive, but errant, young man :

> That not a hurt which in his level came
> Could scape the hail of his all-hurting aim.

L. 12, 'wakened hate' is very strong : there is something serious up be-
tween them.

118

Like as to make our appetites more keen
With eager compounds we our palate urge ;
As to prevent our maladies unseen
We sicken to shun sickness when we purge :
Even so, being full of your ne'er cloying sweetness,
To bitter sauces did I frame my feeding,
And sick of welfare found a kind of meetness
To be diseased, ere that there was true needing.
Thus policy in love, to anticipate
The ills that were not, grew to faults assured,
And brought to medicine a healthful state
Which, rank of goodness, would by ill be cured.
  But thence I learn, and find the lesson true,
  Drugs poison him that so fell sick of you.

To arouse our appetites we sharpen our palates with tart contrasts ; to forestall illness we make ourselves sick with medicine in purging. Even so, being full of your sweetness, though without cloying, I set myself to feed on bitter sauces ; and filled with well-being, I found a kind of meetness in being sick, before there was any need for it. Thus thinking to follow a policy in love, to anticipate ills not yet come, made for real faults and subjected to medicine a healthy state, which — too rich with goodness — would be cured by ill. But thence I learnt a true lesson — that such drugs poison him that in this way sickened of you.

What a curious sonnet, and yet how convincing psychologically ! In such a relationship the moment is apt to arrive when the palate is some-what jaded and needs reviving. The friend (or lover) turns elsewhere, to new acquaintance, new experiences — not necessarily better : indeed Shakespeare does not much relish his choice or his experience :

> To bitter sauces did I frame my feeding.

But he wanted a change, and in this accepts responsibility for his deliberate action. The people whose company he sought were not in themselves very desirable — certainly not in comparison with Southampton. But there was a danger of this relationship cloying : one hears the apprehension beneath the assurance. One feels that when it comes to this, love is coming to an end.

Nevertheless, Shakespeare makes poetry out of it : he turns *everything* to account — it is one of his most salient characteristics from the beginning. And the sonnet, though hardly congenial, is ingenious ; yet the sonnet is true, too, to the facts of Elizabethan life. For the horrors of purging, cf. my *Ralegh and the Throckmortons*, pp. 276-7, 295.

119

What potions have I drunk of Siren tears
Distilled from limbecks foul as hell within,
Applying fears to hopes and hopes to fears,
Still losing when I saw myself to win !
What wretched errors hath my heart committed,
Whilst it hath thought itself so blessèd never !
How have mine eyes out of their spheres been fitted
In the distraction of this madding fever !
O benefit of ill : now I find true
That better is by evil still made better,
And ruined love, when it is built anew,
Grows fairer than at first, more strong, far greater.
  So I return rebuked to my content,
  And gain by ills thrice more than I have spent.

119

What potions have I drunk of woman's tears — distilled from alembics as foul as hell, applying fears to my hopes and then my hopes to fears, ever losing when I thought I was going to win! What miserable errors has my heart committed, while it thought itself never so blessed! How have my eyes been distracted in this mad fever! But I have drawn this benefit from ill: now I find it true that good is bettered by evil, and ruined love, when renewed, grows fairer and stronger than at first. Thus chastened I return to what gives me content, and by the ills experienced gain greatly more than I have lost.

———

Here is the upshot ; here is not artifice, but sincerity. This sonnet makes the transition from the young man to Shakespeare's mistress, and, as we shall see, he comes to speak always of his infatuation for her as a fever, which he does not approve, but cannot help. The 'Siren tears' refers to his mistress ; the alembics 'foul as hell within' obviously not written for her eyes.

Shakespeare's ill experience — we shall see it corroborated in the sonnets dealing with his mistress — brought him back in mind to his friend. And that some good comes from ill is a very Shakespearean thought, constant throughout his work. The theme then is that of *redintegratio amoris*, of love renewed and made stronger for a breach. But — 'ruined love' — I wonder.

L. 14 : editors have followed Malone in altering the original 'ills' to 'ill'. There is no need for this ; indeed it weakens the concrete sense of Shakespeare's ill experiences with the mistress, and I have kept to the original.

120

That you were once unkind befriends me now,
And for that sorrow which I then did feel
Needs must I under my transgression bow,
Unless my nerves were brass or hammered steel.
For if you were by my unkindness shaken
As I by yours, you've passed a hell of time ;
And I, a tyrant, have no leisure taken
To weigh how once I suffered in your crime.
O, that our night of woe might have remembered
My deepest sense, how hard true sorrow hits,
And soon to you, as you to me then, tendered
The humble salve which wounded bosoms fits !
  But that your trespass now becomes a fee :
  Mine ransoms yours, and yours must ransom me.

The fact that you were once unkind is a help to me now, and, as against the suffering which I felt then, I must needs be bent by my transgression, unless my nerves are of brass or steel. For if you were shaken by my unkindness as I was by yours, you've been through hell; and I, like a tyrant, have not had leisure to think how once I suffered for your offence. O, that our night of suffering might have recalled me to my deepest sense — how hard true sorrow hits, and that I have tendered to you, as you did to me, the comfort that befits wounded breasts! But your trespass now becomes something in recompense: mine ransoms yours, as yours must mine.

———

Both Shakespeare and Southampton have been in the wrong against each other, Shakespeare now as his young friend earlier. It is clear that Shakespeare has been neglecting his patron, to whom he owed so much, for the woman in question. We do not know which 'trespass' of Southampton's Shakespeare is here referring to : it may be either his affair with the mistress, or his defection to Marlowe, or both. In spite of Shakespeare's being in the wrong, one has the sense of his feeling of independence, of security, equality, as never in the earlier sonnets.

It is interesting to observe the religious language of the poem — 'transgression', 'trespass', 'ransom' : all of them words that Shakespeare was familiar with from early days in church.

121

'Tis better to be vile than vile esteemed,
When not to be receives reproach of being ;
And the just pleasure lost, which is so deemed
Not by our feeling, but by others' seeing.
For why should others' false adulterate eyes
Give salutation to my sportive blood ?
Or on my frailties why are frailer spies,
Which in their wills count bad what I think good ?
No, I am that I am, and they that level
At my abuses reckon up their own :
I may be straight, though they themselves be bevel,
By their rank thoughts my deeds must not be shown :
    Unless this general evil they maintain —
    All men are bad, and in their badness reign.

121

It is better to be bad than to be thought so, when, if one is not, one has the reproach of being so : there is one's just pleasure lost, condemned not by our own feeling but by other people's opinions. For, why should others' adulterous eyes signalise my wanton ways? Or those even frailer than I spy on my frailties, deliberately putting down as bad what I think good? No, I am what I am, and they that make my ill doings their target expose their own : I may be straight, though they are crooked, my deeds must not be judged by their ill thoughts — unless they hold it as a general view that all men are bad and bent on evil ways.

Of crucial importance autobiographically, for in it Shakespeare tells us what he thinks of himself morally. With absolute honesty he does not hold himself in high esteem. He knows himself too well ; but he also knows other people too well to submit himself, or his pleasures, or his 'sportive blood', to their judgment. Why live our lives in the light of other people's eyes ? He calls theirs 'false adulterate eyes', and regrets any just pleasure lost for their condemnation, not from any real feeling of our own.

There follows the magnificent, quasi-Biblical, affirmation, 'I am that I am', which commands our respect in one with such knowledge of himself — as we have seen, never any excuses, always ready to accept more than his share of responsibility. There is a parallel in *3 Henry VI*, V. vi. 83 : 'I am myself alone'.

L. 11 : the word 'bevel' means sloping, at an angle. No other difficulty, but nearly all the commentators have been bedevilled by humbug over this sonnet and refusing to look it in the face. It is about his affair with his notorious mistress.

122

Thy gift, thy tables, are within my brain
Full charactered with lasting memory,
Which shall above that idle rank remain
Beyond all date even to eternity.
Or, at the least, so long as brain and heart
Have faculty by nature to subsist,
Till each to razed oblivion yield his part
Of thee, thy record never can be missed.
That poor retention could not so much hold,
Nor need I tallies thy dear love to score,
Therefore to give them from me was I bold,
To trust those tables that receive thee more :
    To keep an adjunct to remember thee
    Were to import forgetfulness in me.

122

Your gift, your book, is registered lastingly in my brain — to remain beyond the rank of mere memoranda in a book, even for ever. Or, at least, so long as brain and heart subsist, till each yields up its part of you to oblivion erasing all things, your record will never be wanting. That poor container of a book could not hold so much, nor do I need tallies with which to score up your love : therefore was I so bold as to give your notebook away, to trust those tablets of memory that have more of you. To keep an external aid to remember you would imply forgetfulness in me.

———

Southampton had given Shakespeare a notebook, perhaps with some notes of his own, and Shakespeare has given it away. It seems a curious thing to have done and to need explanation. But Shakespeare is never at a loss, and explains it away : Southampton is so engraved on his memory that he does not need a memoranda-book to remember him by. Ingenious as ever — but the action has the flavour of the end of love to me. The explanation, however, made another subject for a sonnet, when subjects for variation were running short.

The suggestion seems to derive from Ronsard :

> Il ne falloit, Maîtresse, autres tablettes
> Pour vous graver que celles de mon cœur,
> Où de sa main Amour, notre vainqueur,
> Vous a gravée, et vos grâces parfaites.

Perhaps, therefore, Shakespeare's action was notional, to provide a sonnet : it would otherwise be uncharacteristic of him.

123

No, Time, thou shalt not boast that I do change ;
Thy pyramids built up with newer might
To me are nothing novel, nothing strange :
They are but dressings of a former sight.
Our dates are brief, and therefore we admire
What thou dost foist upon us that is old,
And rather make them born to our desire
Than think that we before have heard them told.
Thy registers and thee I both defy,
Not wondering at the present nor the past,
For thy records and what we see doth lie
Made more or less by thy continual haste :
    This I do vow and this shall ever be,
    I will be true despite thy scythe and thee.

Time, you shall not boast that I change ; the pyramids you pile up ever more powerfully are not at all novel or strange to me : they are but elaborations of what has been seen before. Our lives are brief, and therefore we wonder more at things you foist upon us from the past, and rather conceive them shaped to our desire than think them what we have heard of before. I defy both your records and you, wondering neither at the present nor the past, for your evidences and what we see both lie, waxing and waning with your hurried course. This I vow, as it shall ever be : I will be true, despite you and your fell scythe.

———

At first sight it seems that inspiration is running out and that Shakespeare is repeating himself. Ideas and phrases are here from earlier sonnets, yet all the same he gives the theme of time a new twist, even if it is difficult to grasp the not very precise argument. The 'pyramids' in l. 2 have usually been interpreted metaphorically, as all that Time piles up. But I rather think that Shakespeare's mind, concrete and visual, had the fantastic buildings of the age in view — such skyscrapers as Wollaton, Holdenby, Kenilworth, Nonsuch. His preference for what was old is very characteristic of the man, so much of whose inspiration came from the past.

If my dear love were but the child of state,
It might for fortune's bastard be unfathered
As subject to time's love or to time's hate,
Weeds among weeds, or flowers with flowers gathered.
No, it was builded far from accident ;
It suffers not in smiling pomp, nor falls
Under the blow of thrallèd discontent
Whereto the inviting time our fashion calls :
It fears not policy, that heretic,
Which works on leases of short-numbered hours,
But all alone stands hugely politic,
That it nor grows with heat nor drowns with showers.
  To this I witness call the fools of time,
  Which die for goodness who have lived for crime.

––––––––

This difficult sonnet is informative from every point of view, personal and autobiographical, historical and chronological. But the mass of commentary has been more than usually pointless; for it is completely explicable to anyone who knows the circumstances of the time. The poem is politico-religious in its references: 'thrallèd discontent', 'policy', 'heretic', 'politic', 'crime', 'child of state'. In 1594–5 the government's campaign against the Jesuits reached its culmination with the execution of a larger number than at any time for the rest of the reign. The Parliament of 1593 had passed two statutes tightening up the laws against Catholic recusants, for retaining the Queen's subjects in obedience, and against seminary priests reconciling her subjects to Rome. The second Act, 35 Eliz. Cap. 11, refers to the 'wicked and seditious persons who, terming themselves Catholics and being indeed spies and intelligencers not only for her Majesty's foreign enemies but also for rebellious and traitorous subjects born within her Highness's dominions, and hiding their most detestable and devilish purposes under a false pretext of religion and conscience...' There is the point of the sonnet's last line: 'the fools of time, which die for goodness who have lived for crime'.

124

If my love were merely politic it might be thought a bastard love, as subject to time's love or hate, a flower gathered with flowers, or a weed among weeds. But no: it was not built upon chance circumstance; it is not affected by prosperity, nor does it fall under the blows with which discontent is kept down, to which the time is prone. It is not prudential—a heresy in love—to operate on leases of a few short hours, but stands up on its own in monumental state, affected neither by fair weather nor foul. In witness I call those dupes of the age, who die as martyrs, but are condemned for crime.

They died as martyrs for religion, but the Elizabethan government's view was that the Jesuits in particular, involved as some of them were in conspiracies against the state, constituted a fifth column in wartime. Shakespeare reflects the ordinary point of view of people in general in this matter: he thought such martyrs 'the fools of time'.

Southampton was a Catholic, though a politically respectable one, received at Court and not involved at this time in any treasonable activities. But he was not regarded with favour by the Queen or Burghley, and it was on his coming of age in 1594 that he was made to pay—according to the Jesuit, Henry Garnet—an immense sum for refusing to marry Burghley's grand-daughter. So Southampton was at this time under the blows of fortune—this is the current of thought at the back of the sonnet; it reminds Southampton that Shakespeare's love was not founded on chance and was not subject to the ups and downs of fortune. It is so like his prudent mind—for it was in fact prudential—to write so indirectly about 'the blow of thrallèd discontent whereto the inviting time our fashion calls' and to be no more dangerously specific.

Nevertheless, the Sonnets—and the closeness of the relationship—were shortly to end.

125

Were't aught to me I bore the canopy,
With my extern the outward honouring,
Or laid great bases for eternity,
Which prove more short than waste or ruining?
Have I not seen dwellers on form and favour
Lose all and more by paying too much rent
For compound sweet; foregoing simple savour,
Pitiful thrivers in their gazing spent?
No, let me be obsequious in thy heart,
And take thou my oblation, poor but free,
Which is not mixed with seconds, knows no art
But mutual render, only me for thee.
    Hence, thou suborned informer! a true soul
    When most impeached stands least in thy control.

This last sonnet in the Southampton sequence is most suggestive, appropriate to the conclusion of so memorable a relationship. In l. 1, the word 'canopy' suggests the person of honour to whom all the sonnets have been written —

    To one, of one, still such, and ever so.

The theme of the first quatrain is that the external honouring of his young lord meant little to Shakespeare — he had seen too much of life to attach importance to that. The second quatrain reflects on such persons as he had observed, hangers-on of the great, foregoing simple satisfactions for doubtful expectations, throwing away all they have on their hopes — pitiful thrivers, thriving not at all.

The third quatrain gives us Shakespeare's final statement of his own case: his offering to Southampton is 'poor but free', and it is again revealing that at this moment his mind goes back to his country origins: his oblation is not 'mixed with seconds', *i.e.* the second-class flour after the best has been used. And he can conceive of the relationship only on a basis of mutual exchange and equality, 'only me for thee'.

125

Were it anything to me that I bore the canopy over you, with my exterior honouring the outward man ; or laid foundations for eternity, which prove more brief than letting run to waste or go to ruin ? Have I not seen those who hang upon appearances lose all by paying too much for complex expectations, forgoing simple tastes — poor thrivers, utterly spent out in hopes ? No, let my devotion be of the heart : take my offering, poor but free, which is not mixed with seconds and knows no art but mutual exchange, only me for you. Away with those thoughts! a true soul when most maligned with them is least under their influence.

———————

    In the last couplet, 'thou suborned informer' carries on the imagery from the previous sonnet — from the paid informers who spied on the Catholics and betrayed them. Here it is only an apostrophe to the imaginary source of the base thoughts in the first quatrain. There may, however, be a suggestion that Shakespeare felt maligned ('impeached') of just such thoughts as those by Southampton. They would be a natural enough suspicion in such a relationship ; the reply is also obvious — that it is just when one is most suspected of such considerations that one is least influenced by them.
    It may be so.
    It is with this sonnet that the most extraordinary sequence in literature properly ends. We have come full circle from the deference and dependence of the early sonnets to the complete independence and assertion of equality of this.

126

O thou, my lovely boy, who in thy power
Dost hold Time's fickle glass, his sickle, hour :
Who hast by waning grown, and therein show'st
Thy lovers withering as thy sweet self grow'st :
If Nature, sovereign mistress over wrack,
As thou goest onwards still will pluck thee back,
She keeps thee to this purpose that her skill
May time disgrace and wretched minutes kill.
Yet fear her, O thou minion of her pleasure :
She may detain, but not still keep, her treasure !
Her audit, though delayed, answered must be,
And her quietus is to render thee.

O you, my lovely boy, who hold in your power Time's hour-glass and his sickle — you who wane as you grow older and in that show your friends withering as you yourself grow up : if Nature, sovereign mistress over chaos, as you go onwards will ever pluck you back, she keeps you to demonstrate her power to hold up time. Yet fear her, you who are Nature's darling : she may detain her treasure, but not keep it for ever. Her last account, though delayed, must be paid and her discharge is to render you up.

———

This poem of twelve lines in rhymed couplets may be taken to mark the end of the Southampton sonnet-sequence. Turning it into prose brings out, more clearly, if anything, that it is of the nature of an *envoi* : it sums up what may be regarded as the dominant theme, Time and its ineluctable destruction of beauty, and, by implication, of human relationships.

The commentators have made a great hash of ll. 3-4: not one has been able to take Shakespeare's 'who has by waning grown', directly and simply, meaning that the young man's beauty wanes as he grows older. The meaning of ll. 3-4 becomes simple and straightforward, and not in contrast or apposition : as the youth's beauty wanes, so his friends wither as he grows older. Shakespeare's concern with the ebb and flow of things, their waxing and waning, their growing by waning, and renewing by wasting, is very Ovidian: the chief school influence that remained with him all his life.

L. 5: the use of the word 'wrack' is paralleled in both *Venus and Adonis*, l. 558, and *Lucrece*, ll. 841, 966. In the last line the word 'quietus' comes from the old Latin inscription on an account, *quietus est*=he is quit.

127

In the old age black was not counted fair,
Or if it were it bore not beauty's name ;
But now is black beauty's successive heir,
And beauty slandered with a bastard shame :
For since each hand hath put on nature's power,
Fairing the foul with art's false borrowed face,
Sweet beauty hath no name, no holy bower,
But is profaned, if not lives in disgrace.
Therefore my mistress' eyes are raven black,
Her eyes so suited, and they mourners seem
As such who, not born fair, no beauty lack,
Slandering creation with a false esteem :
    Yet so they mourn, becoming of their woe,
    That every tongue says beauty should look so.

―――――

We have to think of Sonnets 1-126 as a continuous sequence, in an intelligible order ; and I think the remaining sonnets, in which Shakespeare's relationship with his mistress is the dominant theme, are so too : they unfold a developing story. But, in time, they interpose themselves into the midst of the Southampton sequence — naturally, for their story is mixed up with his in the triangular relationship that came to be formed.

This sonnet, with its emphasis on women's painting, recalls Sonnet 67, and is closely paralleled by *Love's Labour's Lost*, IV. iii. 249 foll., where Berowne, who is Shakespeare's portrayal of himself, says:

    No face is fair that is not full so black . . .
    O, if in black my lady's brows be decked,
    It mourns that painting and usurping hair
    Should ravish doters with a false aspect ;
    And therefore is she born to make black fair.

256

127

In former times black was not accounted fair, or, if it were, it was not called beautiful; but now black is the proper heir to beauty, and beauty itself is slandered as artificial. For since every hand has assumed nature's power, making foul into fair with borrowed art, beauty herself has no name or refuge sacred to her, but is profaned, if not disgraced. So it is that my mistress's eyes are raven-black, so too brows and eye lashes, and they seem to mourn that those who possess beauty, though not born fair, slander creation by being held in false esteem. Yet they mourn so becomingly that every tongue says beauty should look like that.

Love's Labour's Lost was written in 1593, which gives us a dating for this sonnet and helps us with its argument.

In Elizabethan days black was not counted beautiful, in women's hair, eyes, etc. But now since the rise of painting it is difficult to tell, dark is turned into fair by artificial means: so beauty is not herself, is profaned and driven into retreat. Therefore Shakespeare affirms that his mistress has dark eyes and hair, her eyes seeming to mourn that being beautiful, though not fair, the admiration her beauty attracts is thought misplaced.

L. 10, 'her eyes so suited': no commentator seems to have hit on the sense of that. Yet one should always remember Shakespeare's visual imagination: the meaning is literal and refers to the suit of black around her eyes — eyelashes, brows, hair all black: like Berowne's Rosaline in *Love's Labour's Lost*, who is clearly the dark mistress of the Sonnets.

128

How oft when thou, my music, music play'st
Upon that blessèd wood whose motion sounds
With thy sweet fingers, when thou gently sway'st
The wiry concord that mine ear confounds,
Do I envy those jacks that nimble leap
To kiss the tender inward of thy hand ;
Whilst my poor lips, which should that harvest reap,
At the wood's boldness by thee blushing stand.
To be so tickled they would change their state
And situation with those dancing chips,
O'er whom thy fingers walk with gentle gait,
Making dead wood more blest than living lips.
   Since saucy jacks so happy are in this,
   Give them thy fingers, me thy lips to kiss.

128

How often when you, my music, play music upon that lucky wood whose movement resounds to your fingers, when you gently sway the stringed concord that subdues my ear, I envy those jacks that leap up nimbly to kiss your hand's tender palm — while my poor lips, which should be reaping that harvest, stand by you blushing at the wood's boldness. To be so tickled they would like to change place with those dancing chips, over whom your fingers walk so gently, making dead wood more fortunate than living mouth. Since saucy jacks are so happy, give them your fingers and me your lips to kiss.

What a pretty picture this conjures up of the poet standing politely, but hopefully, beside the lady at the virginals — for the dark lady is evidently musical. It is interesting to compare this sonnet with that written on music to Southampton, Sonnet 8 :

> Music to hear, why hear'st thou music sadly ?
> Sweets with sweets war not, joy delights in joy :
> Why lov'st thou that which thou receiv'st not gladly,
> Or else receiv'st with pleasure thine annoy ?

One cannot but note the contrast in feeling between the one and the other. Though both the lady and the young man are addressed as music — 'my music', 'music to hear' — one observes how appropriate the sentiment of one is for a woman, the other for a young man. We must remind ourselves that these sonnets, though concerned with the lady, came to Southampton : they were the productions of *his* poet.

129

The expense of spirit in a waste of shame
Is lust in action ; and till action, lust
Is perjured, murderous, bloody, full of blame,
Savage, extreme, rude, cruel, not to trust ;
Enjoyed no sooner but despisèd straight,
Past reason hunted, and no sooner had
Past reason hated, as a swallowed bait
On purpose laid to make the taker mad,
Mad in pursuit and in possession so,
Had, having, and in quest to have, extreme ;
A bliss in proof, and proved, a very woe,
Before, a joy proposed, behind, a dream.
 All this the world well knows, yet none knows well
 To shun the heaven that leads men to this hell.

129

Lust in action is the spilling of spirit in a waste of shame ; and till action, lust is perjured and cruel, bloody and savage, extreme, guilty, not to be trusted ; no sooner enjoyed than despised, past reason hunted, and no sooner had than past reason hated, as a swallowed bait laid on purpose to make a man mad, both in pursuit and in possession ; had, having, and seeking to have, without bounds ; the act itself bliss, as soon as over, regretted ; before, a joy proposed, afterwards, a dream. All this the world very well knows, yet no one knows how to avoid the heaven that leads men to this hell.

This virtuoso piece was probably suggested by Philip Sidney's sonnet on the same subject. Sidney is rather less explicit, and in consequence less powerful.

People hardly realise the full subtlety in Shakespeare, that such a sonnet as this — always taken straight and rather heavily — is, in a sense, in inverted commas. It is a literary exercise, but it is also experience. We may imagine the pleasure such a poem gave Southampton and the young men among whom it was handed about.

It is illuminating to compare it with *Lucrece*, ll. 211 foll., Tarquin's reflection :

> What win I if I gain the thing I seek ?
> A dream, a breath, a froth of fleeting joy.
> Who buys a minute's mirth to wail a week,
> Or sells eternity to get a toy ?
> For one sweet grape who will the vine destroy ?

Lucrece was written 1593, the date of the affair with the Dark Lady. It was the dark side of that experience that entered into the poem, with its perturbed and gloomy atmosphere, its moral self-questionings and self-reproach, and marks it off from the gaiety and insouciance of *Venus and Adonis* of the previous year. L. 14, 'hell' has a secondary bawdy meaning, cf. Sonnet 144, l. 12.

130

My mistress' eyes are nothing like the sun,
Coral is far more red than her lips' red ;
If snow be white, why then her breasts are dun,
If hairs be wires, black wires grow on her head.
I have seen roses damasked, red and white,
But no such roses see I in her cheeks ;
And in some perfumes is there more delight
Than in the breath that from my mistress reeks.
I love to hear her speak, yet well I know
That music hath a far more pleasing sound ;
I grant I never saw a goddess go :
My mistress, when she walks, treads on the ground.
   And yet, by heaven, I think my love as rare
   As any she belied by false compare.

130

My mistress's eyes are not at all like the sun; coral is of a far better red than her lips; if snow is white, then her breasts are brown; if hairs are wires, hers are black wires. I have seen damask-roses, mingled red and white, but I do not see such roses in her cheeks; some perfumes give more delight than the breath that comes from her. I love to hear her speak, yet I know quite well that music sounds far better; I never saw a goddess walk, I grant, but when my mistress walks she treads on the ground. And yet I think my love as rare as any woman belied by false comparisons.

This is even more of a literary exercise, and must have given more amusement to Southampton and his friends. For the poem can hardly have been presented to the dark lady, even as a joke. It is a skit on the unreal comparisons, the unconvincing deifications of their mistresses regular with the poets of the sonnet-sequences. In these the women are all goddesses, and nearly all the poets, even Spenser, refer to their hair as golden wires: the new art of head-tiring with wire, the curling and frizzing, made this a fashionable comparison. Shakespeare pokes fun at all these improbable comparisons: his mistress is not a goddess but a real woman, and she treads — do not forget the secondary suggestion — on the ground. And we learn that her hair was black, which some commentators have doubted.

131

Thou art as tyrannous, so as thou art,
As those whose beauties proudly make them cruel ;
For well thou know'st to my dear doting heart
Thou art the fairest and most precious jewel.
Yet, in good faith, some say that thee behold
Thy face hath not the power to make love groan :
To say they err I dare not be so bold,
Although I swear it to myself alone.
And to be sure that is not false I swear,
A thousand groans but thinking on thy face,
One on another's neck, do witness bear
Thy black is fairest in my judgment's place.
   In nothing art thou black save in thy deeds,
   And thence this slander, as I think, proceeds.

You are as tyrannical, even as you are, as those whose beauties make them cruel through pride ; for you know well that to my doting heart you are the fairest, most precious jewel. Yet, in good faith, some people beholding you say that your face has not the power to make love sigh : I dare not be so bold as to say they err, although I swear it alone to myself. And to be sure that what I swear is not false, a thousand sighs one upon another, when I but think on your face, bear witness that your black is fairest in my judgment. You are black in nothing save in your deeds — whence this slander takes its rise.

————

This sonnet brings us nearer to sincerity and the real situation. In fact, there is nothing in the whole sonnet-literature like the realism of Shakespeare's portrait of this woman. No illusion about himself or her. Now that we know who and what she was, we are not surprised to learn that her deeds too were 'black' ; yet Shakespeare is under her spell : to him her 'black is fairest'.

132

Thine eyes I love, and they, as pitying me,
Knowing thy heart torments me with disdain,
Have put on black and loving mourners be,
Looking with pretty ruth upon my pain.
And truly not the morning sun of heaven
Better becomes the grey cheeks of the east,
Nor that full star that ushers in the even
Doth half that glory to the sober west
As those two mourning eyes become thy face.
O, let it then as well beseem thy heart
To mourn for me, since mourning doth thee grace,
And suit thy pity like in every part.
    Then will I swear beauty herself is black,
    And all they foul that thy complexion lack.

132

I love your eyes and they, out of pity for me, knowing your heart disdains me, have put on black and look on me as mourners, showing a pretty compassion for my pain. And truly the morning sun does not better become the grey cheeks of dawn, nor does the star of evening do half that glory to the sober west as those two mourning eyes become your face. O, let it then as well befit your heart to mourn for me, since mourning graces you so well, and wear your pity alike in every part. Then I will swear beauty itself is black, and all that are not of your complexion foul.

Artificial as this is, it represents a further step in Shakespeare's infatuation. The lady is not in love with him, but her beautiful black eyes, which have the appearance of mourning, seem to take pity on him. It is a pretty comment that the moment Shakespeare is in love, he contradicts the sentiments of Sonnet 130 against false comparisons, for here the lady is compared to the morning sun and the evening star. We may take it as confirmation that he *is* in love. A pun on 'mourning' and 'morning', of course, runs all through the sonnet. It is amusing to observe similar verbal tricks that were doing duty for Southampton in the parallel sonnets turned with equal facility and ingenuity á propos of the lady.

133

Beshrew that heart that makes my heart to groan
For that deep wound it gives my friend and me !
Is't not enough to torture me alone
But slave to slavery my sweet'st friend must be ?
Me from myself thy cruel eye hath taken,
And my next self thou harder hast engrossed :
Of him, myself, and thee I am forsaken,
A torment thrice threefold thus to be crossed.
Prison my heart in thy steel bosom's ward,
But then my friend's heart let my poor heart bail ;
Whoe'er keeps me, let my heart be his guard,
Thou canst not then use rigour in my gaol.
    And yet thou wilt, for I, being pent in thee,
    Perforce am thine and all that is in me.

133

Curse that heart that makes my heart groan for the deep wound it gives my friend and me ! Is it not enough to torture me, without enslaving my dearest friend ? Your cruel eye has taken me from myself and engrossed my other self even more : I am deprived of him, myself, and you — a thrice threefold torment thus to be thwarted. Imprison my heart in your breast of steel, but then let my poor heart bail out my friend's ; whoever has me in durance, let my heart guard him : you cannot then make my imprisonment harsh. And yet you will, for I, being pent up in you, am yours perforce and all that is within me.

The sincerity deepens with the situation, for the mistress has got hold of the young man, 'engrosses' him — a course of action she does not choose to employ with Shakespeare : Southampton is a far better catch. We are back at the situation described in Sonnets 34 and 35 in relation to the young man. Here we have Shakespeare's view of it in relation to his mistress. We observe, with some little cynicism, that the mourning eyes, the 'loving mourners', etc. of the previous sonnets have become 'thy cruel eye'. No commentator seems to have unravelled the meaning of l. 11 :

> Whoe'er keeps me, let my heart be his guard.

But surely it is to be taken simply and literally ? — guard meant guardhouse, *i.e.* let my heart keep him. Nor are the last three lines easy : what is meant is — if I may keep him, then my imprisonment may not be rigorous. Yet it will be, for since I am pent up in you, so is all that is in me, *i.e.* my friend too.

134

So, now I have confessed that he is thine
And I myself am mortgaged to thy will,
Myself I'll forfeit, so that other mine
Thou wilt restore to be my comfort still.
But thou wilt not, nor he will not be free,
For thou art covetous and he is kind ;
He learned but surety-like to write for me,
Under that bond that him as fast doth bind.
The statute of thy beauty thou wilt take,
Thou usurer that put'st forth all to use,
And sue a friend 'came debtor for my sake :
So him I lose through my unkind abuse.
   Him have I lost ; thou hast both him and me ;
   He pays the whole, and yet am I not free.

134

Now that I have confessed he is yours and I am myself mortgaged to your will, I am ready to forfeit myself if only you will restore that other mine to be my comfort. But you will not do so, nor will he be free, for you are covetous and he is kind. He learned but as security for me to write on my behalf, and under that obligation is now bound as fast himself. You will take advantage of your beauty, since you are a usurer putting all to use, and sue a friend who engaged himself for my sake ; so I lose him through my abuse of him. I have lost him ; you have both him and me ; he pays the whole debt, and yet I am not quit.

This adds something important to the story of the relations of the three. We learn that to advance his suit with the lady, Shakespeare had got his young friend to write on his behalf, and this was how Southampton had become entangled. He was now in fast ; the lady would naturally prefer such a choice morsel to the poet, so that Shakespeare has (temporarily) lost them both. L. 2 : we are introduced to the double suggestion of the word 'will', which plays such a part in these sonnets, meaning not only desire but sex. L. 11 is elliptical for 'And sue a friend who became debtor for my sake'.

135

Whoever hath her wish, thou hast thy will,
And will to boot, and Will in overplus:
More than enough am I that vex thee still,
To thy sweet will making addition thus.
Wilt thou, whose will is large and spacious,
Not once vouchsafe to hide my will in thine?
Shall will in others seem right gracious
And in my will no fair acceptance shine?
The sea, all water, yet receives rain still
And in abundance addeth to his store:
So thou, being rich in will, add to thy will
One will of mine, to make thy large will more.
    Let no unkind, no fair beseechers kill:
    Think all but one, and me in that one will.

135

Whoever has her wish, you have your will, and will at need,
and Will in overplus : for I am more than enough in plaguing
you, thus adding one more to your sweet will. Won't you, whose
will is large and spacious, condescend once to hide my will in
yours ? Shall will in others seem very acceptable and mine gain no
acceptance ? The sea, all water, goes on receiving rain and adds to its
store in abundance : so you, being very receptive, add to yours one
will of mine, to make your large will more. Let no fair suitors be un-
kindly refused : think them all one and include me in that one will.

———

Now that we know the facts behind the Sonnets and the sense in which the
Elizabethans used the word 'will', this sonnet — never hitherto interpre-
ted — becomes completely clear. The difficulty lay in the first two lines,
which now can be seen to mean: the lady has her sex, her husband,
and Will Shakespeare in addition. This sonnet, which has given the
commentators pages of embarrassed headache, must have given much
amusement to Shakespeare's young friends, and perhaps to the 'lady'
too.

There was an Elizabethan phrase, 'a woman will have her will', which
the sonnet plays upon.

136

If thy soul check thee that I come so near,
Swear to thy blind soul that I was thy Will,
And will, thy soul knows, is admitted there:
Thus far for love, my love-suit, sweet, fulfil.
Will will fulfil the treasure of thy love,
Ay, fill it full with wills, and my will one.
In things of great receipt with ease we prove
Among a number one is reckoned none.
Then in the number let me pass untold,
Though in thy store's account I one must be ;
For nothing hold me, so it please thee hold
That nothing me, a something sweet to thee.
   Make but my name thy love, and love that still,
   And then thou lovest me, for my name is Will.

136

If your conscience upbraids you that I come so near, bid it shut its eyes and say that I was your Will; for will in conscience, is admitted there : thus far for love, fulfil my love-suit. Will will fulfil your love's treasure — certainly, fill it full with wills, so long as mine is one. In things of great capacity we easily prove that one hardly counts among a number. Then let me pass uncounted among the number, though I must be one in reckoning your store ; hold me for a little thing so that it please you to hold that little me, a something sweet for you. Make but my name your love and continue to cherish it, and then you love me, for my name is Will.

The meaning is not difficult to follow, once the veil of humbug is removed from the eyes. The Victorians, however, kept it steadily applied to theirs. With the result that Professor Dowden, usually perceptive, was able to gloss ll. 9-10 as meaning, 'you need not count me when merely counting the *number* of those who hold you dear, but when estimating the *worth* of your possessions, you must have regard to me'! While Knox Pooler was able to gloss 'store's account'' as 'the inventory of your property'! Both explanations are mere flummery, of course. 'Store's account' means simply the number of men the lady had accommodated. There are other plays on words throughout the sonnet, 'come', 'things of great receipt', 'hold', 'a something sweet': drop the Victorian humbug and we may laugh as Southampton and his young friends laughed.

137

Thou blind fool, love, what dost thou to mine eyes
That they behold and see not what they see ?
They know what beauty is, see where it lies,
Yet what the best is take the worst to be.
If eyes, corrupt by over-partial looks,
Be anchored in the bay where all men ride,
Why of eyes' falsehood hast thou forgèd hooks
Whereto the judgment of my heart is tied ?
Why should my heart think that a several plot
Which my heart knows the wide world's common place
Or mine eyes seeing this, say this is not,
To put fair truth upon so foul a face ?
  In things right true my heart and eyes have erred,
  And to this false plague are they now transferred.

137

Love, you blind fool, what do you do to my eyes that they behold and see not what they see ? They know what beauty is and see where it lies, yet take what is the worst for the best. If my eyes, corrupted by the partiality of love, are anchored in the bay where all men ride, why have you forged hooks out of the eyes' falsehood to tie up the judgment of my heart ? Why should my heart think that an individual private plot which it knows is common to all the world ? Or my eyes, seeing this, assert that it is not so, so as to impute fair truth to so foul a face ? In matters of truth my heart and eyes have erred, and in consequence are now infected with falseness.

————

After those two sonnets, comic in their approach, we have a serious one, for Shakespeare is seriously involved, and becomes infatuated with the lady, though he has no illusions about her. Neither have we, any longer. Getting to know her better — he cannot help himself — he becomes more and more uncomplimentary. She is a loose woman, a 'bay where all men ride' (the image is from shipping ; 'ride' was the regular Elizabethan nautical term, but here it has a double meaning), 'the wide world's common place'. Such sonnets cannot have been for her eye ; they were for Southampton's. Perhaps they did him some good, and helped him to emancipate himself from her clutches. Perhaps they were intended to help, as well as amuse, him.

138

When my love swears that she is made of truth
I do believe her, though I know she lies,
That she might think me some untutored youth,
Unlearnèd in the world's false subtleties.
Thus vainly thinking that she thinks me young,
Although she knows my days are past the best,
Simply I credit her false-speaking tongue —
On both sides thus is simple truth suppressed.
But wherefore says she not she is unjust ?
And wherefore say not I that I am old ?
O, love's best habit is in seeming trust,
And age in love loves not to have years told.
    Therefore I lie with her and she with me,
    And in our faults by lies we flattered be.

138

When my love swears that she is true I believe her, although I know she is lying, so that she may think me some inexperienced youth, unacquainted with the world's falsities. Thus vainly thinking that she thinks me young, although she knows quite well that I am past my best, pretending simply to credit her lying tongue — so that on both sides the simple truth is suppressed. But why does she not say that she is untrue ? And why don't I say that I am old ? It is best in love to seem to trust, and age in love loves not to have years counted. So I lie with her and she with me, and in our faults we are soothed by lies.

This takes us further into Shakespeare's relationship with the lady : it is purely sexual, utterly unromantic — unlike that with the young lord. Emilia has become his mistress: she was over five years younger, closer to Southampton in age. In this relationship, too, Shakespeare is much the older : it redoubles his consciousness of his age. Hence the mutual hypocrisies on the surface, for underneath there is Shakespeare's honest candour. From the literary point of view there is the uncompromising realism with which he describes it all : it has been said — rightly — that there is no woman like Shakespeare's in all the sonnet-literature of the Renaissance. Most of them are abstractions or wraiths ; this one is of flesh and blood.

139

O call not me to justify the wrong
That thy unkindness lays upon my heart ;
Wound me not with thine eye, but with thy tongue ;
Use power with power, and slay me not by art.
Tell me thou lov'st elsewhere, but in my sight,
Dear heart, forbear to glance thine eye aside :
What need'st thou wound with cunning, when thy might
Is more than my o'er-pressed defence can bide ?
Let me excuse thee : ah, my love well knows
Her pretty looks have been mine enemies,
And therefore from my face she turns my foes,
That they elsewhere might dart their injuries :
    Yet do not so, but since I am near slain
    Kill me outright with looks and rid my pain.

139

Do not ask me to justify the wrong that your unkindness lays upon
my heart ; do not wound me with your eye, but with your tongue ;
use your power direct, not kill me by artifice. Tell me you love
elsewhere, but in my sight, dear heart, forbear to look aside :
why need you deliberately wound when your power over me is
more than my defences can stand ? Let me excuse you : my love
knows well that her pretty looks have undone me, and therefore
she turns her eyes away from me that they may inflict their injuries
elsewhere : do not do so, but — since I am at your mercy — kill
me straight with looks and put an end to my pain.

Sincere, in spite of the literary artifice, but humiliating — Shakespeare has
to accept the fact that she is attracted elsewhere, but begs that she should
not make it so clear in his presence. The phrasing of l. 3 reminds us of *3
Henry VI*, V. vi. 26, 'kill me with thy weapon, not with words'.

140

Be wise as thou art cruel, do not press
My tongue-tied patience with too much disdain,
Lest sorrow lend me words and words express
The manner of my pity-wanting pain.
If I might teach thee wit, better it were
Though not to love, yet, love, to tell me so ;
As testy sick men when their deaths be near
No news but health from their physicians know.
For if I should despair I should go mad,
And in my madness might speak ill of thee ;
Now this ill-wresting world is grown so bad
Mad slanderers by mad ears believèd be.
    That I may not be so, nor thou belied,
     Bear thine eyes straight though thy proud heart go
       wide.

140

Be wise as you are cruel, and do not regard my silent patience with too much scorn, lest grief lends me words, and words express how much I suffer from your lack of pity. If I might instruct you — though you do not love, it were better to tell me that you do ; as peevish sick men on their death-beds hear nothing from their doctors but of recovery. For if I were to despair I should go mad, and in my madness might speak ill of you ; now this world, that wrests everything to the worst, is grown so bad that mad slanderers are believed by mad ears. That I may not be such, nor you slandered, keep your eyes straight ahead, though your proud heart goes astray.

———

Now that we know the kind of woman she was, l. 5 has a certain edge on it. To Elizabethans 'wit' meant intelligence ; 'if I might teach thee wit' — Shakespeare might certainly give her a point or two here. She could not but play him false.

141

In faith, I do not love thee with mine eyes
For they in thee a thousand errors note,
But 'tis my heart that loves what they despise
Who, in despite of view, is pleased to dote.
Nor are mine ears with thy tongue's tune delighted,
Nor tender feeling to base touches prone,
Nor taste, nor smell, desire to be invited
To any sensual feast with thee alone :
But my five wits, nor my five senses can
Dissuade one foolish heart from serving thee,
Who leaves unswayed the likeness of a man,
Thy proud heart's slave and vassal wretch to be :
   Only my plague thus far I count my gain
   That she that makes me sin awards me pain.

141

In truth, I do not love you with my eyes, for they note a thousand defects in you : it is my heart that loves what they disapprove — which, in spite of what it sees, continues to dote. Nor are my ears delighted with the sound of your voice ; nor tender feeling, prone to low tricks, nor taste, nor smell desire to be invited to any sensual feast with you alone. Yet neither my five wits nor my five senses can dissuade one foolish heart from serving you, leaving only the likeness of a man to be your proud heart's slave and vassal. But thus far I count my plague my gain, that she that makes me sin awards me punishment.

More difficult than usual to render in modern English. L. 6, the Elizabethan word 'touch' means 'trick' ; we still have some sense of it in our slang word, to touch a person, i.e. for money. The language of the Dark Lady sequence is far from elevated — in contrast with that to Southampton. Nor has that been noted.

The reference to plague in l. 13, and that in Sonnet 137, l. 14, remind us that we are in the plague year, 1593.

142

Love is my sin, and thy dear virtue hate,
Hate of my sin, grounded on sinful loving.
O, but with mine compare thou thine own state
And thou shalt find it merits not reproving ;
Or, if it do, not from those lips of thine
That have profaned their scarlet ornaments
And sealed false bonds of love as oft as mine,
Robbed others' beds' revenues of their rents.
Be it lawful I love thee, as thou lov'st those
Whom thine eyes woo as mine importune thee :
Root pity in thy heart that, when it grows,
Thy pity may deserve to pitied be.
    If thou dost seek to have what thou dost hide,
    By self-example mayst thou be denied.

142

Love is my sin, and your best virtue dislike — dislike of my sin, grounded as it is in sinful loving. But compare your own state with mine, and you will find it does not deserve reproof ; or, if it does, not from your lips that have profaned themselves and sealed false bonds of love as often as mine, while you have robbed others' beds of their dues. Let me then love you, as you love those whom your eyes woo — as mine importune you : take pity in your heart so that later it may win you pity in return. If you seek to have what you yourself withhold, you may be denied in keeping with your own example.

———————

The Dark Lady sonnets are more difficult to render in modern English than the Southampton sequence, the thought is more tortured, the language more powerful — and less beautiful. The psychological situation, always obviously a real one, is all the more convincing now we can recognise the familiar humiliations of an older person in love with a younger. It was not for this young woman to object to Shakespeare's infatuation on the ground of its being adulterous, considering what she was. Such is the argument : the time would come when she would need pity. In a few years it did, as we know now, cf. my *The Poems of Shakespeare's Dark Lady*.

Impossible to put more psychological complexity and human experience more concisely than in ll. 9-10 :

> Be it lawful I love thee, as thou lov'st those
> Whom thine eyes woo as mine importune thee.

They sum up the insatiable human pursuit of one another.

143

Lo, as a careful housewife runs to catch
One of her feathered creatures broke away,
Sets down her babe and makes all swift dispatch
In pursuit of the thing she would have stay ;
Whilst her neglected child holds her in chase,
Cries to catch her whose busy care is bent
To follow that which flies before her face,
Not prizing her poor infant's discontent :
So runn'st thou after that which flies from thee,
Whilst I thy babe chase thee afar behind ;
But if thou catch thy hope, turn back to me
And play the mother's part, kiss me, be kind.
    So will I pray that thou mayst have thy will,
    If thou turn back and my loud crying still.

143

Just as a careful housewife, running after one of her chickens getting away, sets down her child and hurries after the thing she wants to stop escaping; whilst her child, neglected, follows after, crying to catch her who is bent on following that which flies from her, not caring for her poor infant's feelings : so you run after that which flies from you, whilst I, your child, chase after you far behind. But if you get what you want, turn back to me and play the mother's part, kiss me and be kind. Then I will pray that you may have your will, if you will turn back and console me.

———

In this equivocal situation, with its growing torment and anxiety, it is nice to think that Shakespeare's humour did not desert him : he could see the funny side in himself chasing after the young woman, while she was chasing someone else. He was ready to accept that she should have her 'will' — here is that word again — provided that he might share in her favours. The sage Victorian, Sir Sidney Lee, thought 'the moral somewhat equivocal . . . There is some suggestion of a *ménage à trois*.' I fear there was more than that.

This simple country scene may be said to take place 'behind the barn', in the old American phrase.

144

Two loves I have, of comfort and despair,
Which like two spirits do suggest me still :
The better angel is a man right fair,
The worser spirit a woman coloured ill.
To win me soon to hell, my female evil
Tempteth my better angel from my side,
And would corrupt my saint to be a devil,
Wooing his purity with her foul pride.
And whether that my angel be turned fiend
Suspect I may, yet not directly tell ;
But being both from me, both to each friend,
I guess one angel in another's hell.
    Yet this shall I ne'er know, but live in doubt,
    Till my bad angel fire my good one out.

144

Two loves possess me, the one comforting, the other despairing, which like two spirits tempt me on : the better angel is a man and fair, the worser spirit is a woman dark in looks. To involve me more — my female evil tempts my better angel away from me, and would seduce his purity with her ill pride. And whether my angel be corrupted, though I suspect, I cannot tell directly ; but both being away from me, and each agreeing with the other, I guess that one angel is in the other's hell. Yet this I shall never know, but live in suspicion, till my bad angel fires my good one out.

———

This presents in serious terms the situation rendered humorously in the previous sonnet — in itself enough to show how all these sonnets hang together, and belong to the same period. After the 'will' sonnets we now have variations on the theme of 'hell', turned ingeniously to a conceit with appropriate imagery, 'spirits', 'angels', 'devils', 'fiends'. How clever — and naughty — it all is ! This particular group coheres with Sonnets 40-42 in the Southampton sequence, and deals with the same experience from another angle. In those Shakespeare dealt with it from the point of view of his friendship with Southampton, much more movingly :

> That thou hast her, it is not all my grief,
> And yet it may be said I loved her dearly ;
> That she hath thee, is of my wailing chief,
> A loss in love that touches me more nearly.

In l. 12,

> I guess one angel in another's hell.

Knox Pooler has the absurdity to guess an allusion to the game of barley-break. Hyder Rollins is nearer the mark in seeing in l. 14 the implication in 'fire out' of venereal disease, rampant in Elizabethan society.

145

Those lips that Love's own hand did make
Breathed forth the sound that said 'I hate'
To me that languished for her sake.
But when she saw my woeful state,
Straight in her heart did mercy come,
Chiding that tongue that ever sweet
Was used in giving gentle doom :
And taught it thus anew to greet,
'I hate' she altered with an end,
That followed it as gentle day
Doth follow night who, like a fiend,
From heaven to hell is flown away.
   'I hate' from hate away she threw,
   And saved my life, saying 'not you'.

145

Those lips that Love's own hand made breathed the words 'I hate'
to me that languished for her. But when she saw my sad condition,
mercy came into her heart, chiding the tongue that was accustomed
to be sweet in pronouncing one's doom ; and taught it a new
greeting. She altered 'I hate' with an end that followed it as gently
as day does night, which, like a fiend, is flown from heaven to hell.
'I hate' she threw away from hate and saved my life, adding 'not
you'.

Some have rejected this sonnet as not Shakespeare's, simply because it is
different and in tetrameters. Hyder Rollins is more sensible : 'I see no
especial reason for rejecting 145. The poet need not always have been
harping on his real or his imaginary mistress's blackness and falsity, but
may sometimes have cajoled her with praises of her kindness. He has
pleaded for his lady's pity in 132, 133, 140 and 142, and here she grants it.
Women, if fiction may be believed, not infrequently do so, even when
they are false.'
 Even this is not particularly percipient ; for observe the imagery of
'fiend' and 'heaven and hell' continued from the previous sonnet, that
shows us that this one is quite right where it is. We have observed the
tact and rhythm by which Shakespeare varies his serious pieces by some-
thing in lighter vein. Even with this light, yet unmistakably Shake-
spearean piece — cf. ll. 6-7 — there is a comparison with *Lucrece*, ll. 1534
foll.

> 'It cannot be', quoth she, 'that so much guile' —
> She would have said — 'can lurk in such a look' ;
> But Tarquin's shape came in her mind the while,
> And from her tongue 'can lurk' from 'cannot' took.

146

Poor soul, the centre of my sinful earth,
. . . these rebel powers that thee array,
Why dost thou pine within and suffer dearth,
Painting thy outward walls so costly gay ?
Why so large cost, having so short a lease,
Dost thou upon thy fading mansion spend ?
Shall worms, inheritors of this excess,
Eat up thy charge ? is this thy body's end ?
Then, soul, live thou upon thy servant's loss,
And let that pine to aggravate thy store ;
Buy terms divine in selling hours of dross,
Within be fed, without be rich no more :
    So shalt thou feed on death, that feeds on men,
    And death once dead, there's no more dying then.

———

Another variation, this has been much admired by philosophically-minded critics ; we may instance Santayana : 'this sonnet contains more than a natural religious emotion inspired by a single event. It contains reflection. . . . A mind that habitually ran into such thoughts would be philosophically pious ; it would be spiritual. . . . The Sonnets are spiritual, but, with the doubtful exception of 146, they are not Christian.'

I wonder whether this lofty sentiment does not contain a little philosophical humbug of its own ? I do not feel that the Sonnets are spiritual : they are altogether this-worldly and human, sensual and psychologically subtle — very Renaissance in fact.

It is interesting to find the word 'earth', used for body in l. 1, appearing in this sense in the neighbouring *Love's Labour's Lost*, IV. iii. 69, 'fair sun, which on my earth doth shine', and *Romeo and Juliet*, II. i. 2,

146

Poor soul, the centre of my sinful body, [confound] these rebel powers that envelop you, why do you pine within and suffer want, while painting your outer walls so gaily ? Why, having so short a lease, do you spend so largely upon your fading mansion ? Shall worms, inheritors of this extravagance, eat up what you have spent so much on ? Is this the body's end ? Then, soul, live upon what the body loses, and leave that in want to increase your strength ; purchase eternity by selling worthless hours ; be fed within, care no more for outward glory : so will you feed on Death, as Death feeds on men, and Death once dead, there is no more dying.

> Can I go forward when my heart is here ?
> Turn back, dull earth, and find thy centre out.

In l. 2 it is vexing that the compositor mistakenly repeated 'my sinful earth' at the beginning of the line, from the end of the previous one. The sense demands some such word as 'confound'. In the same line there has been a lot of discussion about the word 'array'. I do not see why : best to take it in its simple, straightforward sense. The last line is famous and much quoted : the sentiment, of course, Pauline.

Perhaps we may compare this with an earlier attempt, Sonnet 114, to catch up with, or express himself in, the new metaphysical fashion.

My love is as a fever, longing still
For that which longer nurseth the disease ;
Feeding on that which doth preserve the ill,
The uncertain sickly appetite to please.
My reason, the physician to my love,
Angry that his prescriptions are not kept,
Hath left me, and I desperate now approve
Desire is death, which physic did except.
Past cure I am, now reason is past care,
And frantic-mad with evermore unrest ;
My thoughts and my discourse as madmen's are,
At random from the truth vainly expressed.
    For I have sworn thee fair, and thought thee bright,
    Who art as black as hell, as dark as night.

147

My love is like a fever, still longing for that which increases the disease, feeding on that which prolongs the illness, to please the sick appetite. My reason, my physician, angry that his prescriptions are not kept, has left me, and desperate I find that desire, which took exception to physic, is death. Now reason is past caring, I am past cure, and frantic with continual unrest ; my thoughts and discourse are like a madman's, at random from the truth. For I have sworn you fair and thought of you as bright, who are dark as night and black as hell.

With this poem we are back with the theme of 'hell' and Shakespeare's familiar vein, concerned not with his soul and death, but with the facts of life. And also there is his double-mindedness. The sonnet may have a literary point of departure from a poem in Sidney's *Arcadia*, ending,

> Sick to the death, still loving my disease ;

at the same time, it is an expression of personal experience. Shakespeare uses his experience as matter for literature so self-awarely that the result sometimes reads like a literary exercise. However, in spite of the exaggeration, one cannot doubt the sincerity of ll. 7-8. On the other hand, so far from l. 12 —

> At random from the truth vainly expressed —

being the case, he expresses his frantic condition with complete control. This is as poets should be, but it is sometimes difficult to know precisely where one has Shakespeare. I hope this may contribute to explaining a characteristic of him as a writer as to which all agree.

148

O me ! what eyes hath love put in my head,
Which have no correspondence with true sight ;
Or, if they have, where is my judgment fled
That censures falsely what they see aright ?
If that be fair whereon my false eyes dote,
What means the world to say it is not so ?
If it be not, then love doth well denote
Love's eye is not so true as all men's : no,
How can it ? O, how can love's eye be true,
That is so vexed with watching and with tears ?
No marvel then, though I mistake my view ;
The sun itself sees not till heaven clears.
    O cunning love, with tears thou keep'st me blind,
    Lest eyes well-seeing thy foul faults should find.

148

What eyes has love put in my head, which do not correspond with true sight ; or, if they do, where is my judgment that judges falsely what they see correctly ? If what my false eyes dote on is fair, what does the world mean to say that it is not ? If it is not, then it shows that love's eye is not so true as all men's. No : how can it be ? How can love's eye be true that is so vexed with watching and weeping ? It is no wonder, then, that I am mistaken in my sight ; the sun itself does not see till heaven clears. O cunning love : you keep me blind with tears, lest clear-seeing eyes should notice your foul faults.

———

Here is Shakespeare repeating himself, yet to give the theme a different twist. L. 6 tells us that other people knew quite well what Emilia was ; so did Shakespeare, but he was blinded by love, or — we should say — sex. One cannot doubt the sincerity of l. 10. In l. 3 note the characteristic apposition, 'Or, if they have', which occurs before in the Sonnets. In l. 8 observe the audacity of the ending with a colon and a 'no'. There has been much dispute about this punctuation, Sir Sidney Lee expressing the view that 'no particular sanctity attaches to this perplexing punctuation'. The punctuation, in fact, is most effective and clear, and necessary to the sense. In l. 13 the gentlemanly Dowden (he was an Irishman) opines that 'here Shakespeare is perhaps speaking of his mistress, but if so, he views her as Love personified' !

149

Canst thou, O cruel, say I love thee not,
When I against myself with thee partake ?
Do I not think on thee when I forgot
Am of myself, all tyrant, for thy sake ?
Who hateth thee that I do call my friend ;
On whom frown'st thou that I do fawn upon ?
Nay, if thou lour'st on me, do I not spend
Revenge upon myself with present moan ?
What merit do I in myself respect
That is so proud thy service to despise,
When all my best doth worship thy defect,
Commanded by the motion of thine eyes ?
   But, love, hate on, for now I know thy mind ;
   Those that can see thou lov'st, and I am blind.

149

Cruel one, can you say that I do not love you, when I take sides with you against myself? Am I not thinking of you when I forget myself for your sake, tyrant as you are? Who that dislikes you do I call friend; and whom do I fawn upon that you disapprove? No: if you frown on me, do I not react immediately with pain and grief? What quality do I respect in myself that is too proud to serve you, when all the best in me worships your very defects, in subjection as I am to your eyes? But love, hate me as you will, for now I know your mind; you love those that can see you as you are, and I am blind.

————

This group of sonnets clearly belongs together; the theme is Shakespeare's infatuation, though without illusions. The theme is the conflict between what his mind tells him and his infatuation. It is pretty clear that the young woman did not want the poet, that she had other lovers, and that for a time she had got hold of Southampton. Evidently the older man did not appeal to her: he had to put up with what he could get. This sonnet reverses the hitherto frequent refrain, with the woman complaining this time that Shakespeare does not care for her. Not caring for him, alas, does not prevent this kind of reproach. She has enemies, who speak ill of her; Shakespeare takes her side, though he knows better. How convincing it all is! — like a modern novel, unlike anything else in Elizabethan sonnet-literature.

L. 5 reflects Psalm 139: 'Do not I hate them, O Lord, that hate thee: and am not I grieved with those that rise up against thee?'

150

O, from what power hast thou this powerful might
With insufficiency my heart to sway ?
To make me give the lie to my true sight,
And swear that brightness doth not grace the day ?
Whence hast thou this becoming of things ill,
That in the very refuse of thy deeds
There is such strength and warrantise of skill
That, in my mind, thy worst all best exceeds ?
Who taught thee how to make me love thee more,
The more I hear and see just cause of hate ?
O, though I love what others do abhor,
With others thou shouldst not abhor my state.
    If thy unworthiness raised love in me,
    More worthy I to be beloved of thee.

150

From what do you derive this extraordinary power to sway my
heart with your very defects? To make me give the lie to what I
see quite clearly, and swear that black is white? Whence this ability
to make bad things seem good, so that in the very refuse of your
deeds there is such assurance that, in my mind, your worst is better
than other people's best? Who taught you how to make me love
you more, the more I hear and see good reason to hate? Yet,
though I love what others abhor, you should not join with others
in abhorring my condition. If your unworthiness raised up love in
me, I am the more worthy to be beloved by you.

———

Now that there is no mystery about the mistress, we see how truthful and
convincing a portrait of her this was. But l. 13 reveals something new :
it was her 'unworthiness', her pitiable situation that aroused Shakespeare's
love. And now we know what that was, v. Introduction.

L. 4 is paralleled not long after in *Romeo and Juliet*, III. v. 18 :

I am content, so thou wilt have it so.
I'll say yon grey is not the morning's eye.

151

Love is too young to know what conscience is,
Yet who knows not conscience is born of love?
Then, gentle cheater, urge not my amiss,
Lest guilty of my faults thy sweet self prove.
For, thou betraying me, I do betray
My nobler part to my gross body's treason:
My soul doth tell my body that he may
Triumph in love: flesh stays no farther reason,
But rising at thy name doth point out thee
As his triumphant prize. Proud of this pride,
He is contented thy poor drudge to be,
To stand in thy affairs, fall by thy side.
    No want of conscience hold it that I call
    Her 'love', for whose dear love I rise and fall.

———

After the previous serious sonnets, we have, for relaxation, this humorous, naughty one. A Victorian scholar found it 'impossible to admit that Shakespeare would, in his own person, address to *any* woman such gross *double-entendres* as are contained in ll. 8-14'. Hyder Rollins comments, with greater respect for truth, 'to which one might reply that the woman in question is represented as a prostitute, who presumably enjoyed grossness'. But we must not conclude that the lady was a prostitute because she was promiscuous. The Edwardian Liberal, J. M. Robertson, described it as 'a highly anomalous sonnet, isolated in tone and purport from all the others, and introducing a grossness nowhere else to be found in the Quarto'. To which Hyder Rollins very properly replies: 'But 20, 138, and 144 are equally gross', and adds, 'the majority of editors and critics pass this sonnet by in silence, and probably most readers fail to understand it.'

304

151

Love is too young to know what conscience is, yet who does not know that conscience is born of love ? Then, sweet cheat, do not upbraid me with my faults, lest it is you who prove guilty of them. For, if you betray me, I betray my nobler part to the flesh ; my soul tells my flesh to triumph in love, and it awaits no further encouragement, but, rising at your name, points to you as the target. Swelling with this encouragement, he is contented to serve you, to stand by you and fall by your side. Do not hold it for want of conscience that I call her 'love', for whose love I rise and fall.

———

I do not propose to explain what most readers should, without hum-bug, understand. The naughty phraseology of the sestet is paralleled not long after in *Romeo and Juliet*, II. i. 23 foll. :

Mercutio :　　　　　　　　　'twould anger him
　　　　　To raise a spirit in his mistress' circle
　　　　　Of some strange nature, letting it there stand
　　　　　Till she had laid it and conjured it down.

Professor Tucker, who opines that 'this composition is one which, from the nature of its contents, might well be let die', nevertheless en-lightens us usefully with the information, to help us with l. 10, that 'flesh is "proud" when it swells'.

152

In loving thee thou know'st I am forsworn,
But thou art twice forsworn, to me love swearing :
In act thy bed-vow broke and new faith torn,
In vowing new hate after new love bearing.
But why of two oaths' breach do I accuse thee,
When I break twenty ? I am perjured most,
For all my vows are oaths but to misuse thee,
And all my honest faith in thee is lost.
For I have sworn deep oaths of thy deep kindness,
Oaths of thy love, thy truth, thy constancy,
And, to enlighten thee, gave eyes to blindness,
Or made them swear against the thing they see.
  For I have sworn thee fair : more perjured I,
  To swear against the truth so foul a lie.

152

You know that in loving you I am forsworn, but you are twice forsworn in swearing love to me, in breaking your promise in bed and making a new breach after a reconciliation. But why do I accuse you of breaking two oaths, when I break twenty? I am more perjured than you, for all my vows are oaths to abuse, and all my faith in you is gone. For I have sworn to your kindness and love, your truth and constancy; and, to lend you light, blinded my eyes or made them swear against what they see. For I have sworn you fair, and am all the more perjured to swear so foul a lie against the truth.

This bodes the end of the relationship, when Shakespeare says,

> And all my honest faith in thee is lost.

It has been a singularly unhappy one, giving little satisfaction to either partner. We learn from this that there had been a reconciliation, followed by a new breach. L. 3 has usually been taken to indicate that the lady was married; this we now know to have been true, but the context here refers to a vow she had given Shakespeare when in bed with him, after a breach. Hence the 'two oaths' breach' with which he charges her. Evidently she did not much care for him, and perhaps this was the end of the relationship, a suitable juncture at which to terminate it. We learn that Forman's experience three years later was no more satisfactory, and his impression of her character even more unfavourable. But he was not a victim of infatuation or under her spell.

We see, then, that these sonnets belong together as a group, carrying on the themes of feverish love, of the conflict between what Shakespeare well knows and what he wants, of lying to himself against the evidence, of faith forsworn. What a story, described with candour, expressing everything, physical as well as mental! Now the woman wants to end it. Full of anguish as it has been, the experience has at least provided a subject. Art redeems life.

153

Cupid laid by his brand and fell asleep :
A maid of Dian's this advantage found,
And his love-kindling fire did quickly steep
In a cold valley-fountain of that ground :
Which borrowed from this holy fire of love
A dateless lively heat, still to endure,
And grew a seething bath, which yet men prove
Against strange maladies a sovereign cure.
But at my mistress' eye love's brand new-fired,
The boy for trial needs would touch my breast :
I, sick withal, the help of bath desired
And thither hied, a sad distempered guest.
    But found no cure : the bath for my help lies
    Where Cupid got new fire, my mistress' eyes.

153

Cupid laid his brand by and fell asleep : one of Diana's maidens took advantage of this and quickly steeped his love-kindling fire in a cold fountain in the valley : which borrowed from this sacred fire a continual heat, to go on for ever, and become a seething bath, which men try as a cure against strange maladies. But Cupid must needs touch my breast with love's brand, new-fired at my mistress' eyes : I, sick with it, desired the help of the bath and went there, a sadly distempered patient. But I found no cure : the bath to aid me is where Cupid got new fire, my mistress' eyes.

This and the following sonnet are two versions of the same theme, and they are not unsuitably placed as a kind of coda to the Dark Lady Sonnets, to which they relate. They serve quite well to round off the affair, which comes to a sudden end — with Emilia breaking off on her side, Shakespeare to the bath — this was the usual Elizabethan phrase for going to Bath — to cure his distemper.

J. W. Mackail was 'inclined to think' that these sonnets 'are not by Shakespeare at all'. There is no reason whatever to doubt that they are his : they bear every mark of his characteristic ingenuity and suggestiveness.

154

The little Love-god lying once asleep
Laid by his side his heart-inflaming brand,
Whilst many nymphs that vowed chaste life to keep
Came tripping by ; but in her maiden hand
The fairest votary took up that fire
Which many legions of true hearts had warmed ;
And so the general of hot desire
Was sleeping by a virgin hand disarmed.
This branch she quenchèd in a cool well by,
Which from love's fire took heat perpetual,
Growing a bath and helpful remedy
For mèn diseased ; but I, my mistress' thrall,
 Came there for cure, and this by that I prove,
 Love's fire heats water, water cools not love.

154

The little god of love, lying once asleep, laid his heart-inflaming brand by his side, whilst many nymphs vowed to chastity came tripping by. The fairest of them took in her hand the fire that had warmed legions of hearts ; and so the generator of hot desire was disarmed, sleeping, by a virgin. She quenched this brand in a cool well near by, which took perpetual heat from love's fire, becoming a medicinal bath for men diseased. But I, my mistress' slave, came there for cure, and by that I prove this : love's fire heats water, water does not cool love.

For what Shakespeare had in mind, ll. 1 and 7, it is interesting to compare *Love's Labour's Lost* of just this time, III. i. 170 foll. :

> This senior-junior, giant-dwarf, Dan Cupid . . .
> Dread prince of plackets, king of codpieces,
> Sole imperator, and great general
> Of trotting paritors.

So much for Mackail.